50 WALKS IN

Essex

50 WALKS OF 2–10 MILES

First published 2002
Researched and written by Katerina and Eric Roberts
Field checked and updated 2008 by Deborah King
Series Management: Bookwork Creative Associates
Series Editors: Sandy Draper and Marilynne Lanng
Series Design Concept: Elizabeth Baldin and Andrew Milne
Designers: Elizabeth Baldin
Picture Research: Lesley Grayson
Proofreader: Pamela Stagg
Cartography provided by the Mapping Services Department of AA Publishing

Produced by AA Publishing
© Automobile Association Developments Limited 2009

Published by AA Publishing (a trading name of Automobile Association Developments Limited,
whose registered office is Fanum House, Basing View, Basingstoke, Hampshire RG21 4EA;
registered number 1878835)

A03627

ISBN: 978-0-7495-6051-5

A CIP catalogue record for this book is available from the British Library.

The contents of this book are believed correct at the time of printing. Nevertheless, the
publishers cannot be held responsible for any errors or omissions or for changes in the
details given in this book or for the consequences of any reliance on the information it
provides. This does not affect your statutory rights. We have tried to ensure accuracy in this
book, but things do change and we would be grateful if readers would advise us of any
inaccuracies they may encounter.

We have taken all reasonable steps to ensure that these walks are safe and achievable by
walkers with a realistic level of fitness. However, all outdoor activities involve a degree of risk
and the publishers accept no responsibility for any injuries caused to readers whilst following
these walks. For more advice on walking safely see page 144. The mileage range shown on the
front cover is for guidance only – some walks may be less than or exceed these distances.

Visit AA Publishing at www.aatravelshop.com

Colour reproduction by Keenes Group, Andover
Printed by Printer Trento Srl, Italy

Acknowledgements
The Automobile Association would like to thank the following photographers, companies and
picture libraries for their assistance in the preparation of this book.

Abbreviations for the picture credits are as follows – (t) top; (b) bottom; (c) centre; (l) left; (r)
right; (AA) AA World Travel Library.

3 AA/N Setchfield; 9 AA/N Setchfield; 16/17 AA/N Setchfield; 33 AA/N Setchfield;
34 AA/N Setchfield; 56/57 AA/N Setchfield; 62/63 AA/N Setchfield; 88/89 AA/N Setchfield;
99 AA/N Setchfield; 111 AA/N Setchfield; 136/137 AA/N Setchfield

Every effort has been made to trace the copyright holders, and we apologise in advance for
any accidental errors. We would be happy to apply the corrections to the following edition of
this publication.

**Essex County
Council Libraries**

am Abbey (Walk 49)

50 WALKS IN

Essex

50 WALKS OF 2–10 MILES

Contents

WALK		RATING	DISTANCE	PAGE
1	HARWICH	✦✦✦	4 miles (6.4km)	10
2	MANNINGTREE	✦✦✦	7 miles (11.3km)	13
3	WALTON-ON-THE-NAZE	✦✦✦	4.25 miles (6.8km)	18
4	WALTON-ON-THE-NAZE	✦✦✦	6.25 miles (10.1km)	21
5	COLCHESTER	✦✦✦	3 miles (4.8km)	22
6	BRADWELL-ON-SEA	✦✦✦	6 miles (9.7km)	24
7	PAGLESHAM	✦✦✦	6.25 miles (10.1km)	27
8	MALDON	✦✦✦	4.25 miles (6.8km)	30
9	HEYBRIDGE BASIN	✦✦✦	6.5 miles (10.4km)	35
10	HADLEIGH	✦✦✦	4.5 miles (7.2km)	36
11	ROCHFORD	✦✦✦	8 miles (12.9km)	38
12	HANNINGFIELD RESERVOIR	✦✦✦	3.5 miles (5.7km)	41
13	DANBURY	✦✦✦	4 miles (6.4km)	44
14	DANBURY	✦✦✦	4.5 miles (7.2km)	47
15	CHELMSFORD	✦✦✦	3 miles (4.8km)	48
16	EARLS COLNE	✦✦✦	6.5 miles (10.4km)	50
17	CASTLE HEDINGHAM	✦✦✦	3.5 miles (5.7km)	53
18	HALSTEAD	✦✦✦	3 miles (4.8km)	58
19	HALSTEAD	✦✦✦	7.75 miles (12.5km)	61
20	BRAINTREE	✦✦✦	5.5 miles (8.8km)	64
21	LANGDON	✦✦✦	3.75 miles (6km)	66
22	WEALD COUNTRY PARK	✦✦✦	5 miles (8km)	69
23	THORNDON COUNTRY PARK	✦✦✦	4.5 miles (7.2km)	72
24	INGRAVE	✦✦✦	3.5 miles (5.7km)	75
25	DAVY DOWN	✦✦✦	4 miles (6.4km)	76
26	WILLINGALE	✦✦✦	3.75 miles (6km)	78
27	PLESHEY	✦✦✦	3 miles (4.8km)	81
28	CHIPPING ONGAR	✦✦✦	6.5 miles (10.4km)	84
29	CHIPPING ONGAR	✦✦✦	5.25 miles (8.5km)	87

Contents

WALK		RATING	DISTANCE	PAGE
30	LITTLE DUNMOW	✦✦✦	3 miles (4.8km)	90
31	GREAT BARDFIELD	✦✦✦	4.5 miles (7.2km)	92
32	THAXTED	✦✦✦	3 miles (4.8km)	95
33	SAFFRON WALDEN	✦✦✦	5.5 miles (8.8km)	98
34	AUDLEY END	✦✦✦	3 miles (4.8km)	103
35	SAFFRON WALDEN	✦✦✦	3.5 miles (5.7km)	104
36	CHIGWELL	✦✦✦	9 miles (14.5km)	106
37	HARLOW	✦✦✦	4 miles (6.4km)	109
38	MATCHING	✦✦✦	3.5 miles (5.7km)	112
39	HATFIELD HEATH	✦✦✦	6 miles (9.7km)	115
40	HATFIELD FOREST	✦✦✦	4.5 miles (7.2km)	116
41	UGLEY	✦✦✦	5.5 miles (8.8km)	118
42	STANSTED	✦✦✦	3.25 miles (5.3km)	121
43	STANSTED MOUNTFITCHET	✦✦✦	5.75 miles (9.2km)	124
44	STANSTED MOUNTFITCHET	✦✦✦	4.75 miles (7.7km)	127
45	RODING VALLEY	✦✦✦	3 miles (4.8km)	128
46	EPPING FOREST	✦✦✦	7.25 miles (11.7km)	130
47	GILWELL PARK	✦✦✦	6 miles (9.7km)	133
48	WALTHAM ABBEY	✦✦✦	7.5 miles (12.1km)	138
49	WALTHAM ABBEY	✦✦✦	1.5 miles (2.4km)	141
50	THEYDON BOIS	✦✦✦	4 miles (6.4km)	142

Rating

Each walk is rated for its relative difficulty compared to the other walks in this book. Walks marked ✦✦✦ are likely to be shorter and easier with little total ascent. The hardest walks are marked ✦✦✦

Walking in Safety

For advice and safety tips see page 144.

Locator Map

Legend

--→	Walk Route	▨	Built-up Area
❶	Route Waypoint	▨	Woodland Area
– – –	Adjoining Path	👬	Toilet
⚘	Viewpoint	Ⓟ	Car Park
•	Place of Interest	🄰	Picnic Area
⌂	Steep Section	)(	Bridge

6

Introducing Essex

Essex is full of pleasant surprises. It has the largest coastline – more than 300 miles (483km) – of any county in England with a fair share of castles, royal connections and scenic valleys and also comfortably combines history with the contemporary. Let's take Colchester, for example, which was built by the Romans and is Britain's oldest recorded town. Its castle contains the largest Norman keep in the country and yet, a stone's throw from here, East Anglia's newest arts centre, firstsite, is currently under construction and promises to put Colchester firmly on the map as Essex's capital of culture.

Development of the Landscape

Tidal estuaries are plentiful and their mudflats offer migrating birds a winter feeding place. Essex was known as the land of the East Saxons and for hundreds of years people from all over Europe settled here, each wave leaving its own distinctive cultural and social mark on the landscape.

Exploring

Although Essex has neither hills nor mountain ranges this county has plenty of other attractions, many of which can only be appreciated on foot. If you climb up the Langdon Hills, explore the Lee Valley, wander along the high ridges of Hainault Forest or trek through ancient woodland such as Hatfield Forest, you will discover that Essex is a diverse and interesting county and has some very pretty villages.

Walking a little off the beaten track will lead you to the rural retreats of deepest Essex, such as the lovely Colne Valley where agriculture plays an important role. Tourism thrives in pleasant little towns like Thaxted and Saffron Walden and seaside resorts such as Walton-on-the-Naze, which retains a certain 'bucket and spade' holiday charm.

There are ancient monuments to explore: the great Waltham Abbey, Greensted, thought to be the oldest wooden church in the world; one of the finest examples of a former motte-and-bailey castle at the delightful village of Pleshey; Hedingham Castle, magnificently preserved and dating from the 11th century. Here in Essex is also the first Christian site founded when in AD 654 St Cedd brought the Gospel to St Peters-on-the-Wall at Bradwell-on-Sea.

The Landscape

The majority of the walks in this book are circular and vary in length from 2 miles (3.2km) to 10 miles (16.1km). They are mainly rural and coastal walks, with welcoming pubs and cafés. One walk, from Theydon Bois to Epping, is linear and easily accessible via London Underground's Central Line.

The Essex landscape is indeed varied, from the high land in the north and west, and the superb views from Danbury and Thorndon Park, to the

PUBLIC TRANSPORT

For train times call anytime on 08457 48 49 50. For services between Fenchurch Street Station and Southend (Walks 21, 23, 24, 25) call 08457 67 87 65. For information on services between Liverpool Street Station and Colchester (Walks 1, 2, 3, 4, 5, 11, 15, 20) Liverpool Street and Cambridge (Walks 33, 34, 35, 37, 42, 43) and Liverpool Street and Chingford (Walk 46) call 08459 50 50 50. For Walks 45, 50, London Underground information is available on 0207 222 1234. Information on bus times and routes is available daily from 7am to 11pm on 0870 608 2608.

flat coastal plains of the Dengie Peninsular, which have a certain raw beauty best appreciated on a cold, windswept day. Also included is a maritime stroll around Harwich and two town walks; one in the footsteps of Romans in Colchester, and the other around the historic sights of the county town of Chelmsford. And for relatively easy walking, there are several country parks offering well-maintained footpaths and recreational and educational facilities. Some of the walks included in this collection, such as the ones in Epping Forest and near Stansted's runway, are easily accessible from London's Liverpool Street Station, but for sheer isolation and a chance to discover the real Essex, don't overlook the invigorating coastal walks described at Paglesham Creek, Maldon and Bradwell-on-Sea.

Whether you are exploring Essex for the first time or know the county well, you are in for a pleasant surprise.

Using this book

INFORMATION PANELS

An information panel for each walk shows its relative difficulty (see Page 5), the distance and total amount of ascent. An indication of the gradients you will encounter is shown by the rating ▲ ▲ ▲ (no steep slopes) to ▲ ▲ ▲ (several very steep slopes).

MAPS

There are 30 maps, covering 40 of the walks. Some walks have a suggested option in the same area. The information panel for these walks will tell you how much extra walking is involved. On short-cut suggestions the panel will tell you the total distance if you set out from the start of the main walk. Where an option returns to the same point on the main walk, just the distance of the loop is given. Where an option leaves the main walk at one point and returns to it at another, then the distance shown is for the whole walk. The minimum time suggested is for reasonably fit walkers and doesn't allow for stops. Each walk has a suggested map.

START POINTS

The start of each walk is given as a six-figure grid reference prefixed by two letters indicating which 100km square of the National Grid it refers to. You'll find more information on grid references on most Ordnance Survey maps.

DOGS

We have tried to give dog owners useful advice about how dog friendly each walk is. Please respect other countryside users. Keep your dog under control, especially around livestock, and obey local bylaws and other dog control notices.

CAR PARKING

Many of the car parks suggested are public, but occasionally you may find you have to park on the roadside or in a lay-by. Please be considerate when you leave your car, ensuring that access roads or gates are not blocked and that other vehicles can pass safely.

Right: A pathway to St Marys Church in Manningtree (Walk 2)

Harwich's Seafarers and Wanderers

An easy town walk discovering Harwich's exciting maritime past.

DISTANCE 4 miles (6.4km) **MINIMUM TIME** 1hr 30min

ASCENT/GRADIENT Negligible ▲▲▲ **LEVEL OF DIFFICULTY** +++

PATHS Town streets and promenade with gentle cliffs

LANDSCAPE Coast, beach, cliffs and town

SUGGESTED MAP OS Explorer 197 Ipswich, Felixstowe & Harwich or 184 Colchester, Harwich & Clacton-on-Sea

START / FINISH Grid reference: TM 259328

DOG FRIENDLINESS Between 1 May and 30 September dogs have to be on lead on promenade and cliff walks

PARKING Pay-and-display car parks at Ha'penny Pier and informal street parking

PUBLIC TOILETS Beside Quayside Court opposite Ha'penny Pier

One of the main gateways to the Continent, Harwich is a must for aficionados of all things maritime. The town lies beside the grey North Sea on an isthmus between Dovercourt and Bathside bays, overlooking the Stour and Orwell estuaries and drew not only invaders and traders to its shores but adventurers and explorers too. In the 12th century a violent storm caused the rivers to break their banks and form the promontory where Harwich stands today. Realising its strategic importance the lord of the manor developed the site into a walled town. You can see the remains of his wall in St Nicholas' churchyard.

The walk begins at the Ha'penny Pier where you can spot ferries sailing to and from Europe. Keeping the sea to your left you'll see traditional inns, such as the Globe, in Kings Quay Street. Such pubs were once stormed by press gangs who kidnapped boys for service in the Royal Navy. Trying to escape, hapless lads would scurry like rats into the labyrinthine passages linking the houses, but many were caught and never seen again.

Famous Visitors

The town has played host to some famous faces too. Sir Francis Drake dropped in on his way to Spain and Queen Elizabeth I stayed here, remarking that 'It is a pretty town that wants for nothing'. Diarist Samuel Pepys was the local MP and Lord Nelson sojourned here with Lady Hamilton. Home-grown boys include Christopher Jones, captain of the *Mayflower*, the ship in which the Pilgrim Fathers sailed from Plymouth to the Americas in 1620. Wander at will and see the quirky, two-wheel man operated treadwheel crane on Harwich Green or climb Redoubt Fort, built to fend off a threatened Napoleonic invasion, for great sea views. Along the seafront is a pair of 19th-century lighthouses. The first is the Low Lighthouse, now the Maritime Museum and the other, just 150yds (137m) inland, is the High Lighthouse. They were built by General Rebow, a get-rich-quick

HARWICH

entrepreneur who charged each ship a penny per ton to come into port. When Rebow got wind that the sandbanks were shifting he craftily sold the lighthouses to Trinity House. On the way to Dovercourt you'll pass Beacon Hill Fort, dating back to Roman times, although the gun emplacements here are of world war vintages. As you round the breakwater there are fine beaches and another pair of cast iron lighthouses mounted on stilts, built to replace the earlier ones at Harwich. They, too, became redundant (in 1917) but serve as yet another reminder of Harwich's seafaring history.

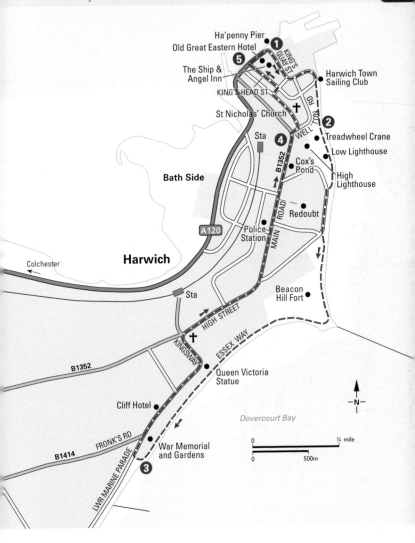

WALK 1 DIRECTIONS

❶ With your back to Ha'penny Pier turn left along The Quay and follow the road into King's Quay Street. Turn left just before the

colourful mural, painted by the Harwich Society and Harwich School in 1982 and again in 1995, which depicts local buildings and ships. Follow the road, with the sea on your left, until it turns

WALK 1

inland. Take the path by the sea, which is the start of the Essex Way, a long distance path of 81 miles (130km) connecting Harwich with Epping. Pass Harwich Town Sailing Club and maintain direction along the Esplanade where at low tide you can walk along the shingle beach.

❷ Pass the Treadwheel Crane on your right and continue along the seafront. Keep the raised, fenced area of Beacon Hill Fort and the gun emplacements from both world wars to your right. As you pass the breakwaters around the bay there are views of the holiday resort of Dovercourt. Ignore the steps to your right and continue along the Essex Way, walking parallel with the upper road of Marine Parade on your right.

WHAT TO LOOK OUT FOR

Look for two quite different walls. One is the Flint Wall in Kings Head Street, made from ship's ballast, and the other is the remains of the 12th-century town wall. The latter is in St Nicholas' Churchyard, opposite the vestry door, where at ground level you can see part of a wall built of septaria, a poor quality stone dredged out of the local estuaries.

❸ Turn right into Lower Marine Parade and pass the War Memorial and Gardens at the junction with Fronk's Road and Marine Parade. Maintain direction passing the Cliff Hotel on the left and then go left into Kingsway, opposite the statue of Queen Victoria. Turn right into the High Street and bear left into Main Road, passing the police station on your left. Walk for 250yds (229m) and turn right up the track to see Redoubt Fort, a Martello-style fort, part of the defences against

WHILE YOU'RE THERE

Visit St Nicholas' Church, built of pale yellow brick in simple Gothic style. Crusaders prayed here before leaving for their journey to the Holy Land; royalty worshipped here on their way to the Continent; and luminaries, such as Willoughby, Drake, Nelson, Samuel Pepys and Daniel Defoe almost certainly visited when they lodged at Harwich.

Napoleonic invasion. Continue to pass Cox's Pond, once owned by local bankers of the same name. They are better known in military circles as Cox and Kings, the Army bankers.

❹ Pass High Lighthouse on the right, turn right into Wellington Road and left into Church Street passing St Nicholas' Church. Turn right into Market Street and left into King's Head Street, pausing to admire the timber-framed houses including No 21, the home of Captain Christopher Jones of the *Mayflower*.

❺ Turn right into The Quay, where Quayside Court faces the sea. Now a block of apartments, Quayside Court was built as one of the Great Eastern hotels in the 19th century and catered for travellers from the Continent who would arrive by steamer at what is now Trinity Quay and continue their journey to London by rail.

WHERE TO EAT AND DRINK

There are plenty of pubs, many dating back to the 16th and 17th centuries including the Angel Inn. There is also the Café on the Pier for light snacks and The Pier at Harwich, right on the seafront with dishes including beef wellington and fresh seafood such as Dover sole and dressed crab salads.

Manningtree – England's Smallest Town

Where the Witchfinder General was born and buried and a Site of Special Scientific Interest.

DISTANCE *7 miles (11.3km)*   MINIMUM TIME *3hrs 30min*

ASCENT/GRADIENT *98ft (30m)* ▲▲▲   LEVEL OF DIFFICULTY ✦✦✦

PATHS *Field paths, footpaths, tracks and sections of road, may be boggy, 4 stiles*

LANDSCAPE *River estuary, undulating farmland dotted with woodland and residential areas*

SUGGESTED MAP *OS Explorer 184 Colchester, Harwich & Clacton-on-Sea*

START / FINISH *Grid reference: TM 093322*

DOG FRIENDLINESS *Can romp free in woodland but must be on lead on farmland and in town*

PARKING *Pay-and-display at Manningtree Station*

PUBLIC TOILETS *Manningtree Station*

On the banks of the River Stour, Manningtree and neighbouring Mistley have long been associated with mills, maltings and timber. In 1753, ships for the Napoleonic Wars were built at Mistley Quay, and Newcastle coal, Scandinavian timber, grain, bricks, chalk, flour and hay were brought down river and transported by barge to London. But these tiny towns, separated by a few miles, are possessed of a darker side... witches!

Matthew Hopkins – Witchfinder General

Cast your mind back to the bad old days of 1644 and imagine reputed witches fleeing from Manningtree's most infamous resident, Matthew Hopkins, better known as the Witchfinder General. If you were female and happened to own a black cat, you risked being branded a witch, to be hunted down by Hopkins' band of distinctly unmerry men. Securing a conviction for witchcraft on the flimsiest of evidence was Hopkins' stock-in-trade, a profession made more unpalatable by the fact that Parliament paid him 20 shillings for each 'guilty' witch. The fate of Hopkins himself is in dispute. Some believe he died a peaceful death at his home in Manningtree in 1647, while others say he was eventually subjected to one of his own witchfinding tests, was found guilty and sentenced to death accordingly. He is believed to be buried in St Mary's Church at Mistley.

This walk starts from Manningtree Station overlooking the River Stour, which separates Essex from Suffolk, and rises to 14th-century St Mary's Church at Lawford to join the Essex Way. It crosses undulating meadows and thick forest – perfect for fleeing witches. A green lane emerges at Mistley where the Swan Fountain is the last surviving example of landowner Richard Rigby's attempts to turn the area into a fashionable spa.

By the end of the 17th century, Mistley and Manningtree were flourishing, busy ports. Malting, Mistley's oldest industry, took off too, and you can still see the chimneys of the English Diastatic Malt Extract

MANNINGTREE

Company (EDME) factory on this walk. If you follow the River Stour, through a Site of Special Scientific Interest (SSSI), back to Manningtree you may spot a large colony of swans, attracted by the waste of the maltings, and other estuary birds including shelduck, teal and ringed plover.

At Manningtree, many of the roof beams of the delightful shops and houses in the High Street date back to Elizabethan times. The witches are long gone, or so they say, and it's hard to believe that between 1644 and 1646 up to 300 victims were rounded up in these parts. Hopkins sometimes held court at local inns, but most of his victims were sent for trial at the notorious Chelmsford Assizes, and many were tried on the evidence of children. Those found guilty were either burnt at the stake or hanged, some of them here on Manningtree's tiny green.

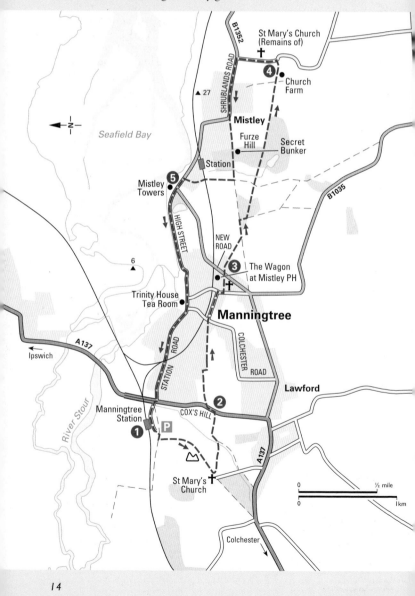

WALK 2 DIRECTIONS

1 With your back to the station building turn right at the public footpath sign to Flatford and after a few steps turn left along a steep, grassy path to St Mary's Church. Go through the black gate and, keeping the church on your right, cross the stile over the church wall. Turn left and, at the wooden post, follow the yellow waymark half right across the meadow. Cross the earth bridge over Wignell Brook, then go left uphill. Keep the line of trees on your right and go through a kissing gate to join the Essex Way. Just before the house at the top of the hill, go through another kissing gate and bear left to Cox's Hill, on to the A137.

2 Cross Cox's Hill with care, turn left and after 40yds (37m), at a public footpath sign marking the Essex Way, turn right. Walk downhill passing to the right of a pond and cross the plank bridge over a stream. Bear right to join the gravel path through the Owl's Flight Dell Conservation Area and pass to the right of a housing estate. Ignoring the concrete path on the left, turn half right on to the cross-field path towards playing fields and join a concrete path to the road. Cross Colchester Road, and at the T-junction turn right into Trinity Road, ignoring signs for the Essex Way. At the Evangelical church turn left between houses to New Road.

The Wagon at Mistley pub is on the left.

3 Cross New Road and follow the yellow waymarked footpath between backs of houses. At the T-junction turn left on to the wide canopied bridleway. After 70yds (64m) follow the waymark half right and rejoin the Essex Way. Maintain direction, go through a kissing gate, cross an earth bridge over the brook followed by a stile and another kissing-gate. Keep ahead through the thickly wooded slopes of Furze Hill. As you emerge from the woods, go straight ahead keeping to the field-edge path to Church Farm. Turn left here on to Heath Road.

4 Cross the road to the low wall to see the remains of St Mary's Church. Continue north and turn left on to the B1352 and into Shrublands Road which soon becomes a green lane. Cross the first stile on the right towards the EDME malt chimney and walk under the railway. Keep ahead into The Green.

5 Turn left into the High Street, past Mistley Towers, and continue beside the River Stour into Manningtree. Bear left along the High Street and continue for 1 mile (1.6km) along Station Road to the car park.

WHAT TO LOOK OUT FOR

In Manningtree look for fine examples of weavers' cottages in Brook Street and South Street and, suspended against a tower, an effigy of the Manningtree Ox, immortalised in Shakespeare's *Henry IV*.

WHERE TO EAT AND DRINK

In Manningtree, you can stop for lunch and a refreshing pint at The Wagon at Mistley in New Road. Vegetarian options and a selection of teas can be had at Trinity House Tea Room in the High Street – the profits go to a local initiative called Acorn Village, which helps people with disabilities.

Overleaf: Furze Hill, Manningtree

Waltzing Around Walton-on-the-Naze

*A day beside the Essex coast exploring
a town with two seasides.*

DISTANCE 4.25 miles (6.8km)   **MINIMUM TIME** 2hrs

ASCENT/GRADIENT Negligible ▲▲▲   **LEVEL OF DIFFICULTY** ✚✚✚

PATHS Grassy cliff paths, tidal salt marsh and some town streets

LANDSCAPE Cliffs, sandy beaches, creeks and marshes

SUGGESTED MAP OS Explorer 184 Colchester, Harwich & Clacton-on-Sea

START / FINISH Grid reference: TM 253218

DOG FRIENDLINESS Take care on narrow paths along cliffs

PARKING Pay-and-display at Mill Lane and Naze Tower

PUBLIC TOILETS Mill Lane and Naze Tower

In the early 19th century Walton-le-Soken, as Walton-on-the-Naze was then known, emerged as a seaside resort attracting fashionable folk from London and county families from Essex, who used bathing machines to dip their toes in the waters. The first terraced houses brought genteel residents, a hotel provided visitors with accommodation and before long the area became as popular as Southend with a pier packed with pastimes. Although Walton's name has since changed, two neighbouring villages, Kirby-le-Soken and Thorpe-le-Soken, still retain the original suffix.

Holiday Resort and Wildlife Haven

Nowadays visitors can enjoy amusement arcades, tenpin bowling, restaurants and sea fishing, and the holiday atmosphere is complete with kiss-me-quick hats, jellied eels and seaside rock. But if you wander north of the town and its lovely wide sandy beaches, you'll discover a haven for bird life in the John Weston Nature Reserve, named after a local warden, and a multitude of sailing craft tucked in the creeks.

Under Threat from Erosion

Part of the town is situated on a headland called The Naze, hence its name. The word originates from the Anglo-Saxon 'ness' or 'naes' meaning a headland, while Walton may mean 'walled town' from the sea wall. Natural erosion has played a big part in the development of Walton-on-the-Naze, although some would class it as terrifying destruction. In 1798 Walton's second church was washed away and at low tide they say you can still hear the bell ring; in 1880 its first pier was destroyed by heavy seas; World War Two gun emplacements and pill boxes built on the Naze itself fell on to the beach and in the next few years, the Naze Tower, a Grade II listed building, which is only just 100yds (91m) from the cliff edge will also be at risk.

Conservationists predict that unless coastal erosion is stopped, or at least slowed down to managable levels, then the area known as the Walton backwaters and home to thousands of birds, seals and other wildlife, will disappear along with a large part of Walton itself. It may come as no surprise that even the lifeboat here lacks a permanent mooring. In fact it is the only lifeboat in Britain to have a mooring in the open sea. It is near the end of the pier and, when the alarm is raised, the lifeboat crew cycle the length of the pier and use a small launch to reach it.

Choose a summer's day for this gentle walk, which takes you through the town and along the seafront to the Naze Tower. You can walk along the beach or along the promenade depending on the tidal conditions. Year round, Walton-on-the-Naze is a delight to explore. In winter you'll see waders and a range of wildfowl, including brent geese and, in summer, you may be lucky to spot rare avocets, which breed here. They have unusual upturned bills which they sweep through the water collecting shrimps and worms.

WALK 3

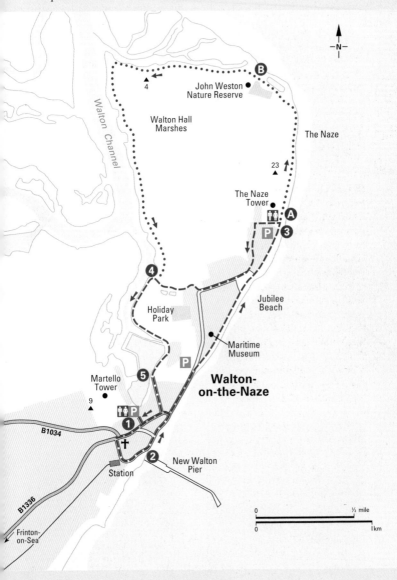

WALTON-ON-THE-NAZE

WALK 3 DIRECTIONS

1 From Mill Lane car park turn right into the High Street then left into Martello Road. Bear left along New Pier Street and go on to Pier Approach. To your right is the Pier, its 0.5 mile (800m) length makes it the second longest in England, after Southend. From here there are good views of the beaches of Walton-on-the-Naze and Frinton.

2 Turn left and, with the sea on your right, walk along Princes Esplanade through East Terrace at the end of which is the Maritime Museum. Continue walking along Cliff Parade and the cliff tops to Naze Tower. Built by Trinity House in 1720 as a navigational aid, it was to join many Martello towers which were built along the east and south-east coasts to fend off Napoleonic invasion. Nowadays, the grassy area in which the tower stands is a good place to rest and recuperate with a hot drink and a picnic at the wooden tables.

3 From the car park café walk inland to Old Hall Lane, turn left and then right into Naze Park Road. At the end of Naze Park Road, where it bears sharp left, turn right on to the narrow path and left on to the field-edge path passing two small ponds filled with wildlife.

4 After 100yds (91m), turn left on to the cross path, go through the gate and on to the permissive path which follows the sea wall, keeping the caravan site on your left and Walton Channel on your right. This wide expanse of mudflats, islands, channels and small boats, ever changing with the tide, is a paradise for seabirds and a Site of Special Scientific Interest (SSSI). Skippers Island, an Essex Wildlife Trust nature reserve, is the habitat of rare seabirds and wildlife and full-time wardens are employed to protect them. Follow the sea wall for 0.75 mile (1.2km) then bear half left down the embankment and into a field used as an overflow car park.

5 With the school field on the left follow railings for 70yds (64m) to a path between the school and terraced cottages and continue to Saville Street past old cottages on your right. Take the first right into North Street, continue to the High Street and turn right. Turn right again into Mill Lane to the car park.

WALTON-ON-THE-NAZE

The Salt Marshes and Seabirds of Hamford Water

A longer loop walk taking in an exhilarating cliff path and nature reserve.

See map and information panel for Walk 3

WALK 4

DISTANCE 6.25 miles (10.1km) MINIMUM TIME 3hrs

ASCENT/GRADIENT Negligible ▲▲▲ LEVEL OF DIFFICULTY ✦✦✦

WALK 4 DIRECTIONS
(Walk 3 option)

From the car park by the Naze Tower, Point **Ⓐ**, follow the path along the cliff edge, though not too close as it is rapidly eroding. The weather and tides have caused the local red clay and shingle to slide away from the flaky London clay underbed. Much of this can be seen if, at low tide, you take the path along the beach; this is also the route for fossil finds. It's easy to ignore the problems of erosion when you look around at the natural beauty of this meeting of wild land and open sea.

Back on the cliff top, continue along the path past large clumps of elder scrub and gorse bush where you may catch a glimpse of small birds such as linnets and goldfinches. As the path slopes downhill the wide Stour estuary comes into view, with Harwich and Felixstowe in the distance. Be careful here, the path nears the cliff edge with gorse on your left, but in another 100yds (91m) the path reaches sea level where there is access to the beach and,

particularly at low tide, mudflats and rock pools – a haven for small children and their grandparents.

Follow the path uphill along the grassy bank of the new sea wall.

To your right you can see the remains of the old sea wall, an indication of the level of erosion in recent years. After 300yds (274m) on the landward side, you can see the enclosed area of the Essex Wildlife Trust's John Weston Nature Reserve, Point **Ⓑ**. The embankment provides a fine vantage point to observe the comings and goings of migrating birds. From here on the area is virtually a bird domain. All through the year terns and waders nest on the beaches and the local redshank and shelduck nest on the salt marshes of Hamford Water. This great conservation area stretches as far as the eye can see, across saltings, marshes and islands, some of which are protected by wardens and one of which, Horsey, is inhabited, but is only accessible at low water.

Your walk continues with this vista for 1.25 miles (2km) until you reach the cross path by Foundry Lane to rejoin the Walk 3 at Point **❹**.

21

WALK 5

Colchester – Britain's Oldest Recorded Town

Following Romans and Victorians along Colchester's ancient walls.

DISTANCE 3 miles (4.8km)	MINIMUM TIME 2hrs
ASCENT/GRADIENT 33ft (10m) ▲▲▲	LEVEL OF DIFFICULTY ✚✚✚

PATHS *Town streets*

LANDSCAPE *Castle, town and park*

SUGGESTED MAP *OS Explorer 184 Colchester, Harwich & Clacton-on-Sea*

START / FINISH *Grid reference: TM 992252*

DOG FRIENDLINESS *Museums, castles and shopping centres aren't usually a dog's idea of a good time*

PARKING *Pay-and-display car parks in city centre*

PUBLIC TOILETS *Castle Park beside Hollytrees Museum*

WALK 5 DIRECTIONS

Imagine yourself back in AD 43 as a lonely Briton trudging across the south-east landscape when you spot a huge Roman army marching towards you. They descend on your home town, which they call 'Camulodunum', and before you know it, they make it the capital of Roman Britain endowing it with a theatre, temples and large houses with central heating and running water. Within a few years a fearsome queen called Boudicca turns up with her army and razes the lot to the ground before continuing to London and St Albans. The Romans rebuild the town within a thick defensive wall.

Today Camulodunum is Colchester, a modern town on the A12, sited on the old Roman road which crossed what was to become Essex from the south-west to the north-east and continued to Harwich on the coast. There's little left of those grand houses and the Roman temple is buried beneath Britain's oldest Norman castle in the heart of town, but much of the Roman wall remains. On this walk you can trace the old wall, taking in snippets of Colchester's colourful history along the way.

From St Mary's car park cross the footbridge over the A134, towards the town centre. Go through Balkerne Gate, one of the most impressive town gates in Roman Britain, built around AD 200. Pass to the left of the Mercury Theatre and the Victorian water tower, known locally as Jumbo.

Turn right along North Hill, past the High Street on your left, into

WHILE YOU'RE THERE
Take a guided tour of the castle and visit the foundations, dungeons and ramparts or let the children play with 'touchy feely' boxes containing pottery and other surprises which give an insight into what life was like in Roman times.

COLCHESTER

WHERE TO EAT AND DRINK

There's plenty of choice, but for a trip back in time try the George, a popular 500-year-old coaching inn in the High Street, which offers snacks and meals in its comfortable lounge and brasserie. You could also try Poppy's Victorian Tea Room in Trinity Street. Quaint and popular it serves home-made scones, using a secret recipe – and also has a playful ghost.

Head Street. After 200yds (183m) turn left into Sir Isaac's Walk, a pedestrian area of specialist shops. Turn left into Trinity Street with its Elizabethan timber-framed cottages and stop at Tymperleys Clock Museum. This early 15th-century house, one of the oldest in the town, was the residence of William Gilberd, a scientist, and Queen Elizabeth I's doctor. At the end of Trinity Street is the 1,000-year-old Holy Trinity Church, constructed from Roman bricks and with a triangular Saxon doorway. Turn right here, skirting the church and follow signs to Eld Lane passing Lion Walk and the United Reformed church.

Keeping the church on your left cross Eld Lane and walk under the arch to a lift that leads to the market (open Friday and Saturday) and the car park. Peer over the side and you will see that you are on the old city walls. Take the lift or walk down the steps and continue along Vineyard Street where you can pick up the old wall on your left.

You are now outside the wall. Cross St Botolph's Street into Priory Street where you'll see the remains of 12th-century St Botolph's Priory, a good example of early recycling by craftsmen who, due to the absence of suitable building material, used the remains of Roman buildings. Keeping the Roman wall on your left follow it along Priory Street to East Hill. Turn left and walk to the top of the hill, passing the entrance to firstsite, the new landmark visual arts centre. Here on the right is the keep of Colchester Castle surrounded by the lovely grounds of Castle Park. Walk through the park keeping the castle on your left and note the obelisk at the rear, which marks the site of execution in 1648 of Sir Charles Lucas and Sir George Lisle, who lay siege to the town during the Civil War.

Just past the obelisk take the first exit on the right, go through the alleyway and turn right into Maidenburgh Street. Here, turn left to No 74, where the remains of the Roman theatre are viewable through a glass panel. Continue walking downhill and turn left into Northgate Street, formerly known as Dutch Lane. In the 16th century Dutch Protestants fleeing persecution at home settled here and brought their weaving skills with them. You can see some fine examples of these timber-framed houses on the corner of West Stockwell Street.

At the end of Northgate Street, turn left into North Hill passing a row of 18th-century houses. A little way along on the same side of the road, stop and admire St Peter's parish church with its Victorian clock. Wealthy Victorian merchants improved churches, built new ones and generally contributed to the town's prosperity with the construction of Castle Park, a public library and schools. At the church, cross the road to return to the car park.

Bracing Bradwell-on-Sea

Smugglers, sea walls and a dying nuclear power station.

WALK 6

DISTANCE 6 miles (9.7km)   **MINIMUM TIME** 3hrs

ASCENT/GRADIENT Negligible ▲▲▲   **LEVEL OF DIFFICULTY** ✦✦✦

PATHS Stony and grassy paths with some road walking

LANDSCAPE Mudflats, salt marshes, beach, farmland, sea wall and former nuclear power station

SUGGESTED MAP OS Explorer 176 Blackwater Estuary, Maldon

START / FINISH Grid reference: TM 024078

DOG FRIENDLINESS A beach for a good romp and paddle

PARKING Informal parking at entrance to footpath at East Hall Farm

PUBLIC TOILETS None en route

If you yearn for huge skies, bracing sea air and long yellow sands, with not a lilo or brolly in sight, then this walk is for you. The Dengie (sounds like Benjie) Peninsula, a vast area of pancake-flat marshes and arable farmland, really does seem in a world of its own, its haunting beauty attracting those seeking to escape the stresses of modern city life.

Smugglers' Haunts

The Dengie Peninsula is bounded by the estuaries of the River Blackwater to the north and the River Crouch to the south. Yet for all its isolation, jutting out into the dove-grey waters of the North Sea, it was a place that needed defending. The Romans built a fort where the present Chapel of St Peter's-on-the-Wall stands, one of several along the coast built to fend off raiders. In the 18th and 19th centuries the chapel took on a different role as a hiding place for bands of smugglers, who would use it to store crates of whisky and rum and other contraband. Meanwhile, notable Bradwell residents, such as Hezekiah Staines, played part-time policeman by day and criminal by night, and spread rumours that the chapel was haunted. Maybe it is.

Contraband Course

This walk starts on an isolated pathway leading to the Chapel of St Peter's-on-the-Wall, the oldest church still in use in England and certainly the sole monument to Celtic Christianity in Essex. Built by the missionary St Cedd in AD 654 it is almost entirely made from debris from the Roman fort on which it stands. In 1920 it took on its present name, and since 1948 has attracted pilgrims from all over the world. Each summer, services are held in the simple barn-like interior. If you choose to take this walk on a cold winter's day when the skies are white and the mists cast a ghostly shroud over the bleak windswept marshes, it's a perfect place for taking shelter from the elements. Once through the heavy wooden door you can imagine old smugglers stacking up their ill-gotten goods inside.

BRADWELL-ON-SEA

Perhaps the most obvious landmark on the landscape, as you continue along the sea wall to Bradwell Waterside, are the looming grey blocks of the former Bradwell Nuclear Power Station, visible for miles around. It started life in 1962, but costs of continued operation outweighed its earning potential; it's now in the decommissioning phase of its lifecycle following 40 years of successful generation. The site is being decommissioned by Magnox Electric. You can take refreshment at The Green Man pub, a smugglers' haven in its day, before continuing to Bradwell-on-Sea, in truth a good way from the seaside. And to complete the contraband course, pause at the parish church where miscreants were incarcerated in a tiny square cell, the Cage, or punished at the whipping post.

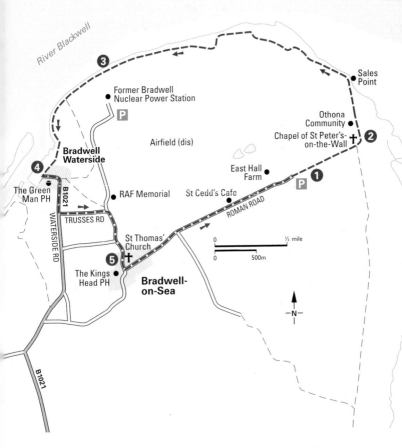

WALK 6 DIRECTIONS

1 Take the wide grassy path from the car park towards the sea and in 0.5 mile (800m) reach the ancient Chapel of St Peter's-on-the-Wall. Continue walking towards the sea for another 30yds (27m) and turn left at the T-junction. After 100yds (91m) climb the wooden steps to the sea defence wall.

2 Keep ahead passing to the right of the religious community of Othona and walk along the wall with the sea on your right. For the next 2 miles (3.2km) your route remains on top of the sea wall, mainly a firm, grassy path punctuated with areas of concrete. On your left, and sometimes seemingly at a lower level to the sea, is private farmland. On your right, salt marsh gives way to white sand and shingle and extensive mudflats at low tide. The seashore makes a lovely detour but at high tide you have to remain on the concrete path. There are good views across the Blackwater estuary to Mersea

club and The Green Man pub on your right. Continue along Waterside Road with the marina on your right. Sean Connery, Bobby Moore and Roger Moore had a hand in turning this marina into a business venture in the 1960s. Continue past the marina and turn left into Trusses Road. Where the road bends, turn right towards Bradwell village (a left turn here towards Bradwell Nuclear Power Station will take you to the RAF memorial at Bradwell Bay Airfield).

❺ At Bradwell-on-Sea follow the High Street to its junction with East End Road where, on the corner, you will find St Thomas' Church opposite The Kings Head pub. Pass Caidge Cottages on your left, the village school on your right and continue for about a mile (1.6km) along the straight Roman Road, with maybe a stop at the Cricketers pub, before reaching the car park.

Island. On the seaward side of the path there are concrete pill boxes, relics of World War Two. The second pill box marks Sales Point, from where there are views of the mooring area used by Thames sailing barges. Follow the path for 1 mile (1.6km) and you can see the framework of the beacon, a good place for spotting swooping cormorants.

❸ In 1.5 miles (2.4km) the bulk of Bradwell Nuclear Power Station is upon you. You may either continue on the route by the coast or make a detour to take in the nature trail around the station. However our route continues along the sea wall to Bradwell Waterside.

❹ At the jetty, turn left on to Waterside Road keeping the yacht

Paddling up Paglesham Creek

A stroll along the sea wall from Paglesham Eastend to Paglesham Churchend, in the footsteps of smugglers and oyster fishermen.

WALK 7

DISTANCE 6.25 miles (10.1km)   **MINIMUM TIME** 2hrs 45min

ASCENT/GRADIENT Negligible ▲▲▲   **LEVEL OF DIFFICULTY** ✦✦✦

PATHS Grassy sea wall, field-edge, unmade tracks, 3 stiles

LANDSCAPE River estuary, salt marsh, mudflats, grazing and arable farmland

SUGGESTED MAP OS Explorer 176 Blackwater Estuary, Maldon

START / FINISH Grid reference: TQ 943922

DOG FRIENDLINESS Big skies and lots of water, but keep on lead along sea wall, where sheep are grazing.

PARKING Informal street parking at Paglesham Eastend beside the Plough and Sail inn

PUBLIC TOILETS None en route

Paglesham, just a few miles from Southend-on-Sea, is bordered to the north by the River Crouch and to the south by the River Roach. Its origins go back to Saxon times and its population survived mainly by rearing sheep that grazed on the flat marshlands. But its remote position on Essex's east coast, and its proximity to waterways, attracted smugglers who would sail up the river bringing in their ill-gotten gains to pass on at a profit to anyone who was happy to make some easy money.

Brazen Blyth

Smuggling was such big business that at one time the entire population of Paglesham was involved in one way or another. In the 18th century one famous resident, William Blyth – also known as Hard-Apple Blyth – was considered to be one of the most notorious smugglers Paglesham ever produced. He started out as the village grocer, progressed to churchwarden and was reputed to have torn up church records to use as wrapping for his butter and bacon. Brazen Blyth would not only evade Customs officials but his party piece was spending evenings at the Punch Bowl pub drinking whole kegs of brandy and crunching wine glasses. This unusual diet and lifestyle clearly did him no harm – he died in 1830, aged 74.

Wife and Oyster Farming

'Wife-farming' seems to have been another popular pastime. Daniel Defoe, in his travels around Paglesham, noted that some men boasted that they had fifteen or more wives. Stories circulated at the time that the women who couldn't stand the rigorous lifestyle and bad weather here, either died from the cold or abandoned their more robust husbands for a more comfortable existence in the uplands from where they originally came. The men simply chose a replacement.

When the villagers weren't smuggling or 'wife-farming' they were engaged in oyster farming, a lucrative business which peaked in the mid-19th century. Oysters were considered common food for Londoners who couldn't get enough of them, and the shortage provided the people of Paglesham with plenty of work. Scores of fishermen would sail out along the estuaries of the Crouch and Roach and return to have their oysters processed by one of the big companies, such as the Roach River Company, now long gone.

On this walk you will see sheep grazing along the grassy sea wall and marshland, just as they have done for centuries, but you'll have to look hard for smugglers in the creeks and estuaries. Oysters are still farmed locally and an annual oyster festival brings a flurry of foodies to the pubs.

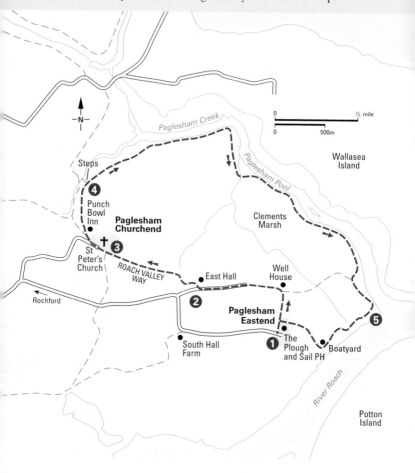

WALK 7 DIRECTIONS

❶ Walk to the left of The Plough and Sail inn along a driveable track, and after 100yds (91m) follow the fingerpost straight ahead to the left of the house called Cobblers Row. Maintain direction along a good field-edge

path, with arable fields either side, until you reach a red brick wall on your left. Go along the lawn of Well House and follow the tarmac lane as it curves left.

❷ At the corrugated barn of East Hall, follow the Roach Valley waymark, right and then left,

PAGLESHAM

WHERE TO EAT AND DRINK

Two pubs provide great food and a smugglers inn atmosphere. Choose between the Plough and Sail at Paglesham Eastend or the Punch Bowl Inn at Paglesham Church End. At the latter, crews of smugglers once played cricket in the nearby field, but would keep their cutlasses and loaded pistols within arm's reach just in case the law caught up with them!

and maintain direction along the good, grassy field-edge. Walk by paddock fencing, with Church Hall on your right and the pond on your left, to St Peter's Church at Paglesham Churchend.

3 Keeping the church on your right, continue along Churchend High Street to the Punch Bowl Inn. Maintain direction for 50yds (46m), take the concrete path to your right soon after the two houses and after a few paces continue along the Roach Valley Way and follow the public footpath sign, left, which soon becomes a grassy field-edge path running parallel with a waterway on your left.

4 Take a short clamber up the grassy embankment and, leaving the Roach Valley Way, turn right on to the sea wall of Paglesham Creek. Keep to the path as it meanders by Paglesham Creek,

which widens as you approach the River Roach. To your left the salt marshes stretch towards the River Crouch where you have views of the marinas of Burnham-on-Crouch and the warehouses and timber yards of Wallasea Island. Much of the landward side of the embankment is given over to sheep grazing which makes this walk somewhat difficult for larger dogs as enclosures are often divided by wooden stiles and low voltage electric fencing.

5 As the path bears right, with the river on your left, maintain direction past oyster beds until you reach the boatyard. Go down the steps from the sea wall and pick your way through boats and machinery to the gate. Pass beside the gate and follow the unmade track until you pass a row of cottages on your left, followed by Cobblers Row and the fingerpost on your right that was the direction for the outward journey. Turn left and return to The Plough and Sail pub at Paglesham Eastend.

WHAT TO LOOK FOR

Paglesham Creek is the habitat of a host of visiting wildfowl. Look for brent geese, black-tailed godwits and shelduck and in winter you may see short-eared owls. You may be lucky and spot insects such as the rare Scarce Emerald damselfly or the Roesel's bush-cricket. In the sea wall look for rare plants such as sea barley and beaked tassel-weed.

WHILE YOU'RE THERE

Paglesham Eastend is home to the delightful OBS cottages, a small row of cottages out of the 120 homesteads in the village. The initials stand for Olivia Bernard Sparrow, a 19th-century benefactor who owned nearby South and East Hall farms. Lady Olivia built the cottages and, with the help of the Revd Herschell, provided schooling for the poor children of the parish.

A Meander Through Maldon

*Combine historic Maldon, home of salt making,
with a network of fascinating waterways.*

DISTANCE 4.25 miles (6.8km)	**MINIMUM TIME** 2hrs
ASCENT/GRADIENT 115ft (35m) ▲▲▲	**LEVEL OF DIFFICULTY** +++

PATHS Mainly grassy paths, narrow in parts and
prone to mud after rain, some roads

LANDSCAPE River estuary, some woodland, canal tow path,
marshland and mudflats, some urban streets

SUGGESTED MAP OS Explorer 183 Chelmsford & The Rodings,
Maldon & Witham

START / FINISH Grid reference: TL 853070

DOG FRIENDLINESS Lots of water but dogs shouldn't take a dip, they
could get stuck in mud. Watch out for Shetland ponies, too

PARKING Pay-and-display car park at Butt Lane

PUBLIC TOILETS Butt Lane

Top television chefs swear by the healthy attributes of sea salt and keen cooks will notice that they often refer to Maldon Sea Salt in their culinary creations. In this walk you'll not only discover picturesque pathways, historic buildings and estuarine bird life, but also pass the factory which has been the home of salt manufacturing since 1882.

A Victorious Battle

Salt aside, it's hard to imagine that the rural riverside town of Maldon, perched on a hill above the River Chelmer, was once the scene of a bloody battle. But one morning, back in AD 991, the Saxon inhabitants awoke to witness 93 Viking longboats sailing up the estuary of the River Blackwater. The invaders, hell-bent on death, destruction and victory, were forced to camp at Northey Island, due to a receding tide which left their ships stranded. Word had spread that Sandwich and Ipswich had been plundered, and under the leadership of Byrhtnoth, Maldon's leader, a two-day battle on the marshes opposite Northey Island ended in a Saxon victory. Byrhtnoth, however, died on the battlefield, his head carried off as a trophy.

Between the 17th and early 19th centuries Maldon thrived as a port town and centre of admiralty jurisdiction due to its position at the head of the Blackwater Estuary. In 1797 the Chelmer and Blackwater Navigation linked the town with Chelmsford. Although Maldon lost out on port dues and maritime trade declined, the town retained its prominence, with the oyster industry and barge trade. It was second in importance only to Colchester, and had already established is own abbey, grammar school and Moot Hall, which later served as a police station, a court and a jail house.

Thanks to the popularity of salt water bathing in the 18th century and the growing barge trade from London, Maldon flourished. By 1847 the town was linked to London by rail and a promenade park attracted wealthy citizens. Ships still come up on the tide bringing grain from Holland to the flour mill on the banks of the River Chelmer and you can also see the traditional Thames sailing barges, identified by their red sails. Many are now given over to pleasure sailing, but in days gone by they plied their trade along the east coast to London.

Today this smart town, with its narrow streets and attractive timber-framed buildings, many with 18th- and 19th-century façades, welcomes the boating fraternity. Landlubbers, more interested in Maldon's social history rather than messing about in boats, can explore the pathways along the River Chelmer or the tow paths of the Chelmer and Blackwater Navigation, which meet in a complex of waterways at Beeleigh Falls.

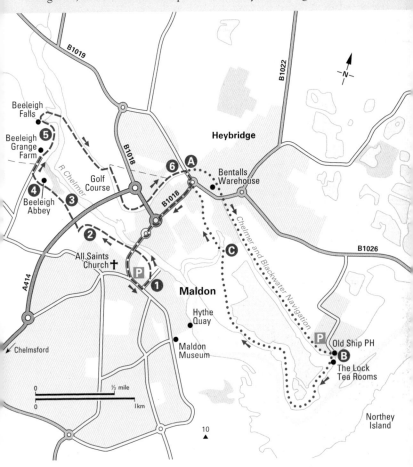

WALK 8 DIRECTIONS

❶ From the car park turn left and walk along Downs Road. The footpath drops quite steeply and soon you have views of the River Chelmer and the salt works. Where the road curves right at the riverside turn left, cross

Fullbridge with care, and follow the grassy embankment keeping the river on your right. Maintain direction and cross a stile. Follow the often muddy path, which meanders uphill through the sloping meadow usually occupied by horses.

WALK 8

❷ Go through a kissing gate and over the adjacent stile and keep ahead, looking out for a stile on the right at the top of the hill. Turn right over the stile. Turn immediately right, along the downhill path through woodland and pass under the A414 Maldon bypass. Continue along the rising concrete path, and at the end turn right.

❸ Maintain direction along this canopied green lane bounded by ancient hedgerows, and cross the stile. Follow the yellow waymark along the grassy path keeping left to emerge on to the gravel path.

❹ On your right is Beeleigh Abbey. Continue past the abbey and at the end of the road turn right. Ignore the footpath on the left and pass Beeleigh Grange Farm on your left, and Beeleigh Falls House, an impressive Victorian villa, on the right. Go through the kissing gate and soon you hear the sound of rushing water of Beeleigh Falls.

❺ Cross the timber bridge over the weir. At the end of the bridge turn right, keeping the river on your right. Stop at the second weir for good river views. Continue, keeping the river on your right, and at Beeleigh Lock turn right and walk, with the canal on your

left, towards the red-brick bridge. Do not cross the bridge, instead turn right on to the concrete path and just before the club house, left on to the grassy path. Maintain direction with the canal on your left and the golf course on your right. Cross the next bridge and turn right, keeping the canal on your right. Continue under two sections of the Maldon bypass and keep ahead on to the grassy bridleway running parallel with the canal.

❻ At the next bridge take the set of steps up to Heybridge Street. At the top turn right and join the B1018 towards Maldon. Maintain direction to cross the River Chelmer via Fullbridge, bear left into Market Hill, turn left into the High Street and return to the car park via Butt Lane on your left.

Right: The River Chelmer at Maldon (Walk 8)

To Heybridge Basin

*A longer loop walk taking in views
of Northey Island and marshlands.*

See map and information panel for Walk 8

DISTANCE 6.5 miles (10.4km)   **MINIMUM TIME** 3hrs 30min

ASCENT/GRADIENT 113ft (35m) ▲▲▲   **LEVEL OF DIFFICULTY** ✦✦✦

WALK 9 DIRECTIONS
(Walk 8 option)

You can extend your walk along the canal to Heybridge Basin and see Northey Island, where in 991 Vikings camped before the Battle of Maldon. Cross Heybridge Street, Point **Ⓐ**, and rejoin the tow path along the Chelmer and Blackwater Navigation. On your left are the cemetery and canal gate. On your right are typical canalside buildings, including Bentalls warehouse built in 1863. William Bentall, a ploughmaker, transferred his business to Heybridge in 1805 to take advantage of the canal.

Walk along the tow path for 1 mile (1.6km), to Heybridge Basin where there are interesting 18th- and early 19th-century pubs and houses. This area replaced Fullbridge on the River Chelmer as the transhipment point for coal and other goods when the canal was completed. Today it is renowned for its expertise in converting barges and fishing boats into pleasure craft.

At the Old Ship public house, Point **Ⓑ**, turn right on to the footbridge over the lock and walk along the embankment. To your left is Northey Island and to your right, across marsh and heathland, are views of Maldon.

Today Northey Island is a Site of Special Scientific Interest (SSSI), and can only be reached at low tide via a causeway. To the east is the privately owned Osea Island, once rumoured to be a hideaway for celebrities.

As you continue towards the town look out for the spire of 12th-century St Mary's Church, which because of its location serves as a navigational aid for incoming shipping. Across the river you will see the attractive Edwardian Park, built in 1895 as a recreational centre for local people and visitors. To the right of the park is Hythe Quay where you'll see several Thames sailing barges with their characteristic sprit sail rigs. Their shallow draft allowed them to sail the muddy creeks and inlets of the Essex and Kent coasts but they became redundant following the development of road transport.

Follow the footpath for about 1 mile (1.6km), Point **Ⓒ**, to industrial installations on your left. Turn left here and almost immediately right along a grassy path which leads into Bates Road. After 500yds (457m) turn left to the B1018 to rejoin Walk 8.

Left: Canal lock at Bridge Beeleigh Falls, Maldon

35

Hadleigh Country Park

A fairly taxing walk with steep green slopes, marshes and a famous castle.

DISTANCE 4.5 miles (7.2km)   MINIMUM TIME 2hrs 15min

ASCENT/GRADIENT 207ft (63m) ▲▲▲   LEVEL OF DIFFICULTY +++

PATHS Woodland and field tracks, grassy paths and some streets

LANDSCAPE Pasture and scrub, salt marsh and woodland

SUGGESTED MAP OS Explorer 175 Southend-on-Sea & Basildon

START / FINISH Grid reference: TQ 800869

DOG FRIENDLINESS Plenty of open spaces but watch for cows around castle

PARKING Pay-and-display parking at Chapel Lane

PUBLIC TOILETS Chapel Lane car park

WALK 10 DIRECTIONS

Modern times may have engulfed much of Hadleigh's history, but in the village centre you can't fail to notice the 13th-century church enclosed, not by a green, but by a busy one-way traffic system. Meanwhile out on the hill overlooking the railway line, linking the Essex coast with London and beyond it the Thames estuary and the Kent countryside, are the ruins of Hadleigh Castle which stand as testimony to a bygone era. Founded by Hubert de Burgh in 1231 as a guard against the risk of attack by France, it was rebuilt by Edward III in the 14th century.

But before you visit the castle, take in part of Hadleigh Country Park. Start this walk from the car park and follow the path through the kissing gate. Turn left, taking the left stepped path downhill to a wide grassy plain, go through a kissing gate and make for the clump of trees on your right. Continue alongside these to cross a track by a 'Hadleigh Castle via Marsh' public footpath sign. Follow the path towards the railway line, and turn left at the waymark. Keep ahead with the railway on your right, until you reach a waymarked path leading up to the castle.

Hadleigh Country Park has been an important conservation area since the 1950s due to its variety of habitats, from grassland and woodland to salt marsh and mudflat. The park covers 472 acres (191ha) and overlooks Canvey Island, the River Thames and the Kent Downs. The area once consisted of two farms, Poynetts and Kersey, which used only traditional chemical-free farming methods. The rich soil sustains a variety of wildlife making this a

WHERE TO EAT AND DRINK

The Crown @ Hadleigh and The Castle both serve traditional pub food and ales but for fine views of the countryside and non-alcoholic drinks with your snack stop at the Salvation Army Tea Rooms at Home Farm.

HADLEIGH

WHAT TO LOOK OUT FOR

Look for the south-east tower at Hadleigh Castle, the highest part of the ruin, for a view of the Thames as seen by landscape painter, John Constable (1776–1837). In 1814, Constable made a sketch of the castle, later used in his work *Hadleigh Castle* (1829).

delightful place to visit; in spring you can see shaded woodlands of bluebells, yellow calandine, nettle-like yellow archangel and plenty of butterflies; in summer you may hear the sound of a cuckoo or spot grass snakes and adders on the rough grass and heathland.

The views of the estuary and the Kent countryside improve with every step as you reach the summit of the hill, where you'll find the impressive remains of Hadleigh Castle. After Hubert de Burgh's death, in 1243, the danger of attack from France decreased and the castle fell into disrepair. It was spruced up again when Edward III came to the throne in 1327. Stone and sand were imported from Kent, chalk and plaster from London, wood and tiles from Thundersley, straw from Benfleet and glass from Rayleigh.

By 1551 the slopes were unstable and the castle suffered from landslip. It was sold to Lord Richard Riche who made a tidy sum selling the stone as building material for houses and churches on his properties in Essex and by 1600 the castle was in ruins.

In the 19th century there were tales of a ghostly woman in white who dislocated the neck of a milkmaid when she refused to meet her at midnight, and of smugglers who sailed up the River Thames, climbed the hill and hid their ill-gotten gains in the ruined castle. Such stories were told in the pubs in Hadleigh where it was also believed that there was a tunnel linking Hadleigh Castle with the Castle Inn.

Having had your fill of folklore you now exit through a gate and turn right, and through a kissing gate into Castle Lane, passing Home Farm, now a training centre for the Salvation Army. In 1890 General William Booth set up a colony here for the rehabilitation of down and outs from London. Some 400 men passed through the establishment, working at various aspects of farming, before either returning to their families, settling down in the local area or seeking pastures new via the Salvation Army's emigration department.

WHILE YOU'RE THERE

Visit Two Tree Island Nature Reserve to the south-east of the castle. Topsoil was brought in to cover this former rubbish dump, which today is a paradise for insects and small mammals. There is a bird hide overlooking the lagoon and marshland, which attract kingfishers, grey herons, avocets and short-eared owls and will appeal to birders.

Walk up Castle Lane and at the top, where it meets the High Street, turn left. Cross the road to visit St James the Lesser Church with its lovely Norman apse. If it is open, look at the 13th-century carved font, but pride of place is taken by a painting of Thomas Becket.

Continue along the High Street and turn left into Chapel Lane and return to the car park.

Rochford – the Place of the Peculiar People

An easy walk along the River Roach following part of the Roach Valley Way and a visit to a tiny medieval town.

WALK 11

DISTANCE 8 miles (12.9km) **MINIMUM TIME** 3hrs

ASCENT/GRADIENT Negligible ▲▲▲ **LEVEL OF DIFFICULTY** ✚✚✚

PATHS Grassy sea wall, field-edge paths and town streets

LANDSCAPE River estuary, salt marsh, mudflats, arable land and urban development

SUGGESTED MAP OS Explorer 176 Blackwater Estuary, Maldon

START / FINISH Grid reference: TQ 875904

DOG FRIENDLINESS A big walk for many dogs with long sections on lead

PARKING Pay-and-display at Back Lane

PUBLIC TOILETS Back Lane car park

Rochford, a small medieval market town, just over 3 miles (4.8km) north of Southend, is worth visiting before or after this walk for its abundance of delightful cottages, many of which are listed buildings. The town centre contains one of the few remaining market town cross patterns in England, comprising North, South, East and West Streets. In 1257, the lord of the manor, Sir Guy de Rochefort, was granted a charter to hold a weekly market, which still takes place every Tuesday in the square.

But there have been horrific, and odd, goings-on in this peaceful town. In 1555 villagers gathered in the square to witness the execution of John Simson, a farm labourer from Great Wigborough. He was burnt at the stake because he refused to conform to Roman Catholicism. A plaque on the wall of a bakery shop commemorates his martyrdom.

Peculiar Experience

A few centuries later in 1837 James Banyard, a shoemaker, had a religious experience which inspired him to form a Christian sect which became known as the Peculiar People. Peculiar to Essex, the sect had its headquarters in Rochford. The group took its name from Deuteronomy, Chapter 14, Verse 2, which proclaims, 'and the Lord hath chosen thee to be a peculiar people unto himself'. Banyard, who took to religion after spending his life as a drunkard, rounded up followers and preached with such fervour that he and his flock were treated with suspicion and hostility.

Even more strange were their dress and customs. The men were clean shaven and wore bowler hats and the women went about their daily business in black bonnets. They rejected orthodox medicine and when one of the sect fell ill, the illness or disease was treated with the laying on of hands, or the affected part or parts would be anointed with oil. Needless to say, not all treatments were successful and there was often an outcry among local people when children from the sect died.

But in 1855, James Banyard's son became ill and, fearing that he would not live, Banyard summoned the doctor. Such disregard of the rules caused a split in the movement and Banyard was ousted. He was duly replaced and the centre of operations moved from Rochford to Daws Heath 5 miles (8km) away. Banyard never regained leadership and presumably went back to shoemaking; he died in 1863.

On this walk you may glimpse the ghost of a black-bonneted lady with her black skirts billowing like a sail on the flat open landscapes. She may disappear as soon as you hear the planes roaring above open fields bound for Southend Airport and if you linger long enough, she may re-appear. There are many peculiar happenings in this peculiar little town.

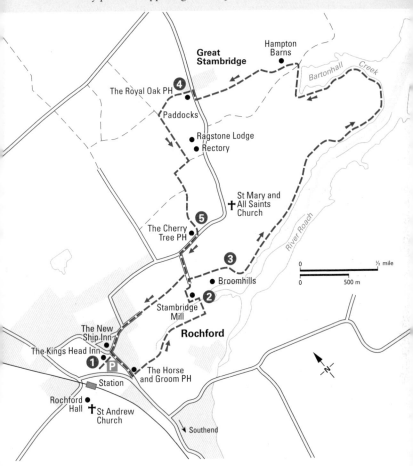

WALK 11 DIRECTIONS

❶ From the car park walk north between houses into Market Square and turn right into South Street, passing the police station on your left. By The Horse and Groom pub, turn left into Watts Lane following the Roach Valley Way through industrial installations and keeping the River Roach on your left for a mile (1.6km).

❷ Follow the path over the bridge, with Stambridge Mill straight ahead. Follow the concrete path around the mill until you reach Mill Lane. Turn left, and after 50yds (46m), turn right on to the cross-field path to the footbridge over the fishing lake. Go through the kissing gate and on to the gravel path. Maintain direction through trees and across the meadow, where on your right you can see Broomhills house, the former home of John Harriot the founder of the Thames River Police.

WHAT TO LOOK OUT FOR

Visit St Mary and All Saints Church at Stambridge with its distinctive square Saxon tower and look for the stained-glass memorial window known as the Winthrop Window. It was placed in the church by the American descendants of Stambridge's most famous resident, John Winthrop who, in 1630, set sail for the Americas in the *Arabella* and went on to become the first Governor of Boston.

3 Follow the waymark through the kissing gate and join the river bank path. With the river mudflats and salt marsh on your right, continue ahead along the grassy sea wall. Look left to see the Saxon tower of the church at Great Stambridge. Continue around the peninsula of Bartonhall Creek, a popular feasting ground of mudflats for migrating birds. As you reach the north-western tip, walk left down the embankment to the fingerpost, leaving the Roach Valley Way, and turn left towards Great Stambridge to pass a number of old Essex barns converted into modern housing. Maintain direction along the field-edge path towards houses and after 0.5 mile (800m) the path passes Ash Tree Court and emerges on the Stambridge Road. Turn right into Great Stambridge past The Royal Oak pub and notice the array of attractive Victorian villas and the post office.

WHERE TO EAT AND DRINK

The Cherry Tree pub is an 18th-century pub with a modern twist and has a good selection of seafood on the menu. It's popular with locals. Other choices include the Kings Head in Market Square and a couple of tearooms in South Street.

4 Just before the post office, turn left into Stewards Elm Farm Lane and follow the waymark over the footbridge. Maintain direction between a series of paddocks until you reach the kissing gate and turn left to follow the field-edge path keeping Ragstone Lodge and the Rectory on your left. Continue on the cross-field path following the waymarks right, left, then half right past houses on your right, until you meet Stambridge Road.

5 Turn right at The Cherry Tree public house and after about 200yds (183m), turn left into Mill Lane, then right, before houses, on to the cross-field path to join Rocheway past the houses and past The New Ship Inn on your right. Turn left into South Street and return to the car park.

WHILE YOU'RE THERE

Continuing the theme of peculiarity in Rochford don't forget to visit St Andrew's Church, the only church in England which stands in the middle of a golf course. Just opposite is Rochford Hall, part residential and part home of the Rochford Hundred Golf Club. The hall stands on the site of the residence of Sir Thomas Boleyn whose daughter, Anne, married Henry VIII in 1533. She was executed three years later, but not before she had given birth to a son, who died, and a daughter who went on to become Queen Elizabeth I.

Roaming Around Hanningfield Reservoir

Birds, wildlife, and a waymarked nature walk through meadows and woodlands.

DISTANCE 3.5 miles (5.7km)   **MINIMUM TIME** 1hr 30min

ASCENT/GRADIENT Negligible ▲▲▲   **LEVEL OF DIFFICULTY** ✦✦✦

PATHS Grassy and gravel forest tracks, prone to mud after rains, some boardwalk

LANDSCAPE Reservoir, forest and grassy meadow

SUGGESTED MAP OS Explorer 175 Southend-on-Sea & Basildon

START / FINISH Grid reference: TQ 725971

DOG FRIENDLINESS No-go area except for guide dogs

PARKING Free parking at the Visitor Centre, Hawkswood Road entrance. Gates close at 5pm

PUBLIC TOILETS Visitor Centre

If you're a birder, or just enjoy nature, then Hanningfield Reservoir and Nature Reserve is the place for you. The south-eastern shores of the 970-acre (393ha) reservoir have been set aside as a nature reserve by the Essex Water Company and are a Site of Special Scientific Interest (SSSI). Managed by the Essex Wildlife Trust, it is best known for the prolific numbers of wintering and breeding wildfowl. Among them are nationally important numbers of coot, gadwall and tufted duck. If you're there in early winter you will also see pintails in large numbers. The chalk-based sludge on the western side of the reservoir supports plants uncommon in Essex, such as golden dock and marsh dock.

Pleasant Strolling

An interesting nature trail leads through the woodland, where there are four especially well-constructed bird hides overlooking the reservoir and banks enabling you to spend all day spotting species such as pochard, shoveler, shelduck and great crested grebe. But for non-twitchers, waymarked trails lead through ancient coppice and secondary woodland, with ponds, hedges and ditches. Pleasant strolls through four different woods, Chestnut, Peninsular, Well Wood and Hawkswood are there to be enjoyed.

Coppiced Woodland

Hanningfield Reservoir was built to provide water for an increased population after World War Two and, in the 1960s, the area which forms part of today's nature reserve, was planted with conifers. Thirty years later, in 1992, the Essex Wildlife Trust took over management of the site and the reserve is, today, renowned for its abundant wildlife. In Chestnut Wood there are areas of Scots pine which have been thinned to allow in light to the cleared sunny grasslands, which are an excellent habitat for butterflies and crickets. Ponds, ditches and piles of dead wood have attracted dragonflies, newts and grass snakes. In Peninsular Wood, near Point and Oak Hides,

HANNINGFIELD RESERVOIR

WALK 12

warblers nest and feed in an area which was cleared and allowed to regenerate as scrub. And in Well Wood and Hawkswood you can see the perimeters of ancient woodlands where coppiced hornbeams and hazel allow the old plant and animal communities to flourish once more.

Spend some time in the Visitor Centre, either before or after your nature walk, to see some novel conservation ideas in action, such as composting toilets which need no flush and a log-burning stove using wood from the reserve. Water is conserved by collecting rain water from a large roof and using it to top up two wildlife ponds beside the Visitor Centre. You can use complimentary binoculars (donation appreciated) to spot dozens of birds feeding at one of these ponds from the viewing gallery inside the centre.

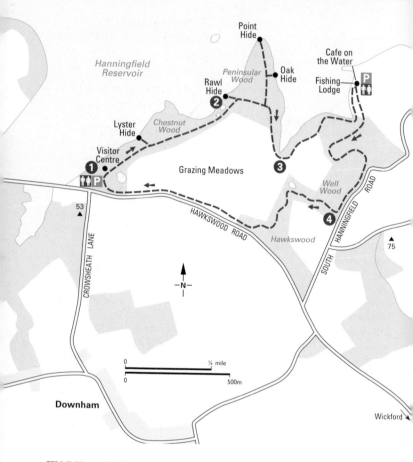

WALK 12 DIRECTIONS

❶ Go through the Visitor Centre, take the path ahead to waymark 1 and detour left for views of the reservoir from Lyster Hide. Return to 1 and continue along the path through Chestnut Wood

for 100yds (91m). At waymark 3, bear right to the clearing with picnic tables and then go straight ahead towards tall oaks and waymark 4. Keep ahead to cross the wooden footbridge, passing the pond on your left, and continue until you reach

HANNINGFIELD RESERVOIR

WHAT TO LOOK OUT FOR

Bluebells cover Well Wood in spring while early summer brings a colourful display of foxgloves and flocks of swifts, swallows and martins feed on newly hatched flies. In autumn and spring, Oak Hide, which looks across to the Fishing Lodge, attracts a good variety of wading birds. In winter the grazing fields buzz with wigeon, teal, geese and swans.

WHERE TO EAT AND DRINK

Pleasant reservoir views, freshly prepared snacks and meals can be had half-way round this walk, at the licensed Café on the Water at the Fishing Lodge. Choose from jacket potatoes, grills and daily specials. Otherwise pack your own picnic and enjoy the views beside the water's edge.

waymark 7 on the edge of the wood. Ahead are grazing meadows. Turn left along the gravel path, keeping the meadow on your right, later following the boardwalk on your right to an outdoor classroom in a clearing with ponds and seating made from split trunks.

❷ At waymark 8 turn left, passing waymark 9 to reach to Rawl Hide, for good views of the reservoir and the reed covered embankment on the left. Now return to waymark 9, turn left on to the wide grassy path to enter Peninsular Wood and continue to waymark 12. Bear left for 100yds (91m) and pass by Oak Hide to maintain direction to the tip of the peninsula and waymark 13, where you'll find Point Hide. Retrace your steps to waymark 12 and turn left in the direction of the Fishing Lodge with the reservoir on your left. Maintain direction

WHILE YOU'RE THERE

You'll need a day permit to fish at Hanningfield Reservoir, but if you don't fancy hooking your catch you can always buy fat trout from the Fishing Lodge. The species comes in all its forms from fresh or frozen to smoked and is sold cleaned whole, filleted or as steaks.

passing waymarks 14 and 15 to cross the concrete bridge.

❸ Ignore the stile across to Hawkswood and bear left to waymark 17 and enter Well Wood. Turn left and continue until you meet waymark 19, with the Fishing Lodge and Water's Edge off to the left. Swing right and walk straight ahead, between coppiced trees with the high embankment on your left denoting the old boundary of the woods, to waymark 18. Turn left, keeping meadows on your right, to waymark 24. Turn left to way-mark 23 and right to waymark 22. Turn right again, into an area of less dense woodland with South Hanningfield Road on your left.

❹ At waymark 25, continue to a clearing of coppiced hornbeams, where the path descends and goes past several small ponds to waymark 26 passing waymark 27. Keep ahead to cross the grassy track and just after waymark 28 bear left to enter Hawkswood. Keep ahead past waymarks 29 and 30 and at waymark 32, turn right cross a wooden footbridge and go through a series of kissing gates to return to the car park.

Places and Palaces in Danbury Country Park

A gentle countryside walk, with panoramic views, exploring ancient woodland, flower-filled meadows and bird-filled lakes.

DISTANCE 4 miles (6.4km)   MINIMUM TIME 2hrs

ASCENT/GRADIENT 164ft (50m) ▲▲▲   LEVEL OF DIFFICULTY ✦✦✦

PATHS Grass and woodland paths, field paths, some road

LANDSCAPE Ancient woodland, lakes, meadows

SUGGESTED MAP OS Explorer 183 Chelmsford & The Rodings, Maldon & Witham

START / FINISH Grid reference: TL 781050

DOG FRIENDLINESS Some open space but must be on lead most of way

PARKING Free car park off Main Road opposite library and inside Danbury Country Park

PUBLIC TOILETS Main Road car park, car parks at Danbury Country Park which also have facilities for disabled

Danbury is surrounded by delightful woodland, much of it common land, and is the largest area of woodland in Essex after Epping Forest. Steep hillocks and heathland soil have prevented intensive arable farming and, as a result, its environs are now designated nature reserves, owned and managed by various conservation agencies, including the National Trust and the Essex Wildlife Trust. These areas pack in a huge variety of habitats in a relatively small space and, if you're a lover of woodland walks, then a stroll around Danbury is bound to appeal.

Diminutive Danbury

The village is perched on a hill, 350ft (107m) above sea level, on the A414 east of Chemsford. The slender spire of St John the Baptist Church is visible for miles around, especially if you're approaching along the A12 from London. This superb setting compensates for what Danbury lacks in historic buildings and, apart from the church, there is little to detain you in the village.

From Place to Palace

On this gentle walk you'll discover some characterful 18th- and 19th-century farms and cottages and the rather splendid 16th-century Danbury Palace, (off limits to the public) inside the country park. Sir Walter Mildmay, founder of Emmanuel College, Cambridge, built the house you see today and called it Danbury Place. But when it was sold to the Church of England in 1845 for £24,700, and occupied by George Murray, 96th Bishop of Rochester, it became known as Danbury Palace, reflecting its change in status.

In the 13th century, aristocratic families went deer hunting in the park, which had been a gift to Geoffrey de Mandeville, 1st Earl of Essex, by William I. Today the country park has three delightful duck-filled lakes,

DANBURY

picnic areas and impressive specimens of beech and oak. Beside the palace there are beautiful ornamental gardens filled, in summer, with flowers from Asia and the Americas, while herbaceous perennials attract butterflies.

Your journey's end is at St John the Baptist Church, in a location where Iron Age farmers once lived. Having risen to these comparatively dizzy heights, look southwards where the views are both impressive and extensive, and you soon understand why the Saxons fortified this position. The Normans, following in their footsteps, built the church and everyone was happy for a time. But, when Henry VIII decreed that the monasteries should be dissolved in 1536, church furnishings throughout the land were sold to avoid confiscation. The story goes that an enterprising medieval DIY enthusiast used much of the wood from the church to kit out The Griffin inn across the road and, until a few decades ago, part of the rood screen could still be seen above the bar.

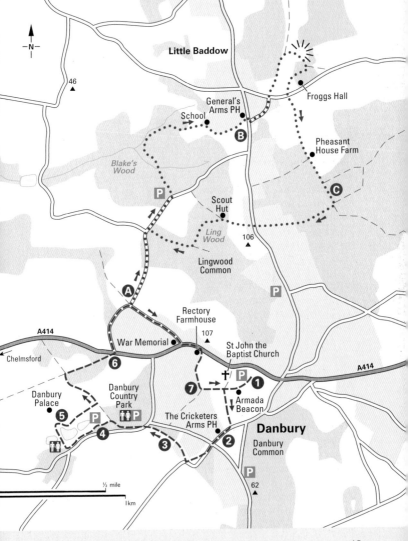

WALK 13 DIRECTIONS

1 Leave the car park via the grassy path to the right of the leisure centre. Bear right along an uphill path beside the hedgerow and at a crossing of paths by a radio mast turn left and head downhill. Ahead are views of south Essex towards Kent.

2 Turn right to pass The Cricketers Arms, then cross Bicknacre Road into Sporhams Lane. Follow the path marked 'Butts Green'. At a signpost on the right, take a track through dwarf oaks and gorse, to cross a plank footbridge. After 25yds (23m), turn right along a track, past houses.

3 At the house called Dane View, keep left and follow the footpath through woodland to Woodhill Road, and turn left to the sign marking the entrance to Danbury Country Park on the right. In the car park take the kissing gate on the left and go left again on to the path just before the information board.

4 Maintain direction past another car park and go through the kissing gate on the left before the bridge. Pass to the left of two lakes and, at the toilets, turn right between lakes and continue ahead to reach the red-brick perimeter

wall of the Danbury Conference Centre and Palace.

5 Turn right through formal gardens and, at the end of the second lake, turn left though trees. Maintain direction uphill, diagonally across a meadow and through the kissing gate. From the kissing gate, walk half left uphill towards the copse. Continue to a crossing of paths taking the one to the right which soon passes to the left of a pond before reaching a meadow. Cross the meadow towards the oak trees, following the red and white posts.

6 At the last white post, turn left and go through a kissing gate carefully on to the busy A414. Cross the road into Riffhams Lane. At Elm Green Lane turn right, uphill, to the A414 by the war memorial on the green. Turn left, cross the road and turn right beside Rectory Farmhouse.

7 At the T-junction turn left for views of St John the Baptist Church and graveyards. At the second T-junction, turn left to visit the church. Turn right to rejoin your outward path and return to the car park.

Danbury Wildlife

*A longer loop to encompass the woods and wildlife
around Danbury.*

See map and information panel for Walk 13

DISTANCE 4.5 miles (7.2km) **MINIMUM TIME** 2hrs 30min

ASCENT/GRADIENT 148ft (45m) ▲▲▲ **LEVEL OF DIFFICULTY** ✦✦✦

WALK 14 DIRECTIONS
(Walk 13 option)

From Point **A** continue along
Riffhams Lane and, at the
junction, bear right into Riffhams
Chase and left into Blakes Wood
car park. Take the path to the
left of the information board,
waymarked 'Wildside Walk',
into a dense area of Blakes Wood
dominated by hornbeam and
chestnut, and which in spring
comes alive with impressive
displays of bluebells. Cross a
footbridge and keep the stream
on your left.

After 300yds (274m) you reach an
area of fallen trees, the result of
storm damage in 1987. The path
now rises again leaving the stream
behind, and you later bear left to
emerge into Colam Lane passing
the school on your left. Follow the
tarmac Parsonage Lane to meet
The Ridge with the General's
Arms pub on the left, Point **B**.

Turn right and take the first left
into Mill Lane. Cross a lane and
follow the footpath to The Old
Rodney, keeping the white house
on your right. Pass the sign for
Heather Hills Nature Reserve
and, at the next public footpath
sign, turn right past viewpoints
across farmland to your left to
continue along the bridleway.
At the next public footpath sign

turn right, passing the fencing
enclosing Froggs Hall on your left.
Continue through woodland and,
after 200yds (183m), cross Spring
Elms Lane to pick up the footpath
to a bridleway, Postman's Lane.
Keep the grazing land of Pheasant
House Farm on your left.

You are now deep in the heart of
the Danbury Ridge, a 240-acre
(97ha) area of long-established
woodlands. Here you may see
green woodpeckers or spot
butterflies hovering on hemp
agrimony. At an information
board, Point **C**, turn right to
reach the residential area of Fir
Tree Lane, cross The Ridge and
pick up the footpath to the right of
the bus stop. Pass the scout hut on
your right, then turn left into Ling
Wood. Turn right at the cross path
to a bench that gives fine views
of Danbury village. Lingwood
used to be grazing land but is now
covered with birch and oak where
the National Trust has maintained
clearings to retain birds, insects
and plants in their natural habitats.
The path continues to Riffhams
Chase where you turn left into
Riffhams Lane to rejoin Walk 13.

Chelmsford City Walk

An easy ramble highlighting some historic buildings.

DISTANCE 3 miles (4.8km)   MINIMUM TIME 1hr 15min

ASCENT/GRADIENT Negligible ▲▲▲   LEVEL OF DIFFICULTY ✚✚✚

PATHS Pedestrianised streets and pavements

LANDSCAPE Historic streets and buildings

SUGGESTED MAP OS Explorer 183 Chelmsford & The Rodings, Maldon & Witham

START / FINISH Grid reference: TL 713067

DOG FRIENDLINESS Pedestrianised areas provide traffic-free walking

PARKING Several pay-and-display car parks in city centre

PUBLIC TOILETS Duke Street

WALK 15 DIRECTIONS

Once a small Roman military settlement on slightly raised ground near the junction of the River Cam and the River Chelmer, Chelmsford was known as Caesaromagus or Caesar's Plain, and was the only place name in Roman Britain to have an imperial prefix. Granted a market charter in 1218, it became the county town of Essex, a position it still holds today.

From the car park in Bond Street head towards the town centre and join the High Street to Shire Hall, site of the assizes and quarter sessions where, 350 years ago, Nonconformists and witches were tried in open court beneath a timber-framed canopy. Today the 18th-century building is used as the Magistrates Court.

Turn left at Shire Hall and take the first turning on the right to England's smallest cathedral. In the grounds, look for the triangular gravestone dedicated to three Marys, Mary Ann Woolmer, Mary Elizabeth Eve and Mary Smith, who perished in a fire which partially destroyed the town in 1808. Note the grim epitaph 'Prepare for death ere ye retire to rest, for ye know not what a day may bring forth'. Parts of the cathedral date back to 1420; on the south-east side is a figure of St Peter holding a Yale key. Walk clockwise around the cathedral passing old sunken gravestones and leave the grounds the same way you came in.

Cross Tindal Square passing the statue of 19th-century judge, Lord Chief Justice Nicolas Tindal, who

WHILE YOU'RE THERE

Two free museums in Oaklands Park, Moulsham Street are the Chelmsford and Essex Museum, for displays of local and social history, including a rare hoard of gold Celtic coins, and the Essex Regiment Museum for military exhibits and a large archive of photographs, letters and diaries.

CHELMSFORD

was born and bred in Chelmsford. Walk along Tindal Street passing Judge Tindal's tavern on the left, to the traffic lights at New London Road. Here, turn right and cross the bridge over the River Cam to Parkway. Just around the corner, beside the subway, an information panel describes the site of a 13th-century Dominican friary. Take the subway and follow the signs for the C & E Hospital. As you emerge the yellow-brick Infirmary and Dispensary is on your right.

Continue past the hospital to where a pathway to the right leads to a statue of Graham Gooch, captain of Essex and England cricket teams. Just past the statue rejoin New London Road via the narrow path on the left and look back to see the front of two Victorian villas, Thornwood and Bellefield. The first mayor of Chelmsford, Frederick Chancellor lived at Bellefield.

Walk on along New London Road for more examples of fine Victorian-style houses and attractive terraced cottages, many of which have been converted into offices. Further up on the left is the delightful Melford Villas and immediately next door is the street's oldest business, Lucking & Sons, funeral directors, which is adjacent to the overgrown Nonconformists' cemetery.

Keep ahead to the crossroads where you will see the building of Essex Radio on your right. Turn left into Elm Road and then left again into Moulsham Street, the site of the old London Road and the former manor of Moulsham, given to Thomas Mildmay by Henry VIII for his role as receiver of monies during the Dissolution of the Monasteries. The street contains many listed buildings, including six almhouses founded by Thomas Mildmay, and rebuilt in 1758. Further along there are shops and cottages where the upper storeys overhang. A particularly good example is No 41, dating from the 15th century.

Where the street ends, cross Parkway via the subway or the pedestrian crossing and continue along Moulsham Street to reach the High Street. Just after Baddow Road, on the right, is the former Regent Playhouse theatre, now a café. At the junction to Springfield Road, the next turning on the right, is the site of the Black Boy Inn, immortalised by Charles Dickens in *The Pickwick Papers*.

Back in the High Street, on the right, is the Royal Bank of Scotland, the former Mansion House and lodgings of the judge when he sat at the assizes. Shire Hall is straight ahead and from here you return to the car park.

WHAT TO LOOK OUT FOR

Look for blue plaques commemorating famous people, on buildings around the town. They include Thomas Hooker, founder of Connecticut in 1636, and others who helped shape Chelmsford's history, such as Guglielmo Marconi, who established the world's first radio factory in New Street.

WALK 16

Along the River Valley to Earls Colne

A fairly challenging walk along a disused railway track, now a nature reserve, and through ancient woodland.

DISTANCE 6.5 miles (10.4km)   MINIMUM TIME 3hrs 30min

ASCENT/GRADIENT 78ft (24m) ▲▲▲   LEVEL OF DIFFICULTY +++

PATHS Grassy with some muddy tracks, forest and field-edge paths, 1 stile

LANDSCAPE Disused railway line, ancient woodland, riverside and grazing meadows

SUGGESTED MAP OS Explorer 195 Braintree & Saffron Walden

START / FINISH Grid reference: TL 856290

DOG FRIENDLINESS On a lead near the kennels

PARKING Free parking at Queens Road car park in Earls Colne

PUBLIC TOILETS Queens Road car park

Is this the loveliest valley in all Essex? Judge for yourself as you follow the meandering River Colne and visit the delightful village of Earls Colne where the de Vere family, Earls of Oxford and one of the greatest families in English history, left their name. Here you will find a lovely view from the split-timber seating beside St Andrew's Church, with its tower visible for miles around; a nature reserve along a disused railway track, which has been cut back allowing wildlife to flourish, and the ancient woodlands of Chalkney Woods.

A Disused Railway Line

The Colne Valley Railway opened in 1860 and soon brought prosperity to the valley. Earls Colne, one of the stations on the line, was built by the Hunt family who developed the Atlas Works, which produced farming equipment until it closed in 1988. The line was used to import raw materials and to despatch the finished product, but since its closure in 1965 the track-side vegetation has become a rich habitat for wildlife, with plenty of trees and shrubs providing heavy shade. As you walk along the disused track you will see evidence of coppicing which allows light to reach the ground, which in turn allows wildlife such as butterflies and other insects to proliferate.

Chalkney Wood dates back to 1605 when it was owned by the de Vere family. This walk takes you through the woods where conifers are gradually being replaced with traditional species. You'll also see, near the kennels, an 18th-century watermill which last worked in the 1930s and is now a private residence. In the Alder Valley are the remains of conifer plantations established in the 1960s, but today the area supports more moss and liverworts than any other wood in East Anglia. You'll also pass close to the Wool Track, believed to be an ancient Roman road linking Colchester and Cambridge, and come across a prominent bank which enclosed the woods as a swine park where pigs would feed on acorns amongst the coppice.

Brickfields and Long Meadow Nature Reserve, bordered by woodland of oak, ash and hawthorn, has plenty of boggy areas and wet grassland. It is small, but has plenty of insect life. The ponds, surrounded by acacia and rhododendron, are home to newts, frogs and dragonflies. A major feature of the area is the anthills, which house huge colonies of yellow ants. Long Meadow, used for grazing, is free of fertilisers and pesticides, and as a result supports plenty of wildlife and a variety of grasses such as yarrow and birds trefoil. Near by you should also find a rare surviving elm tree.

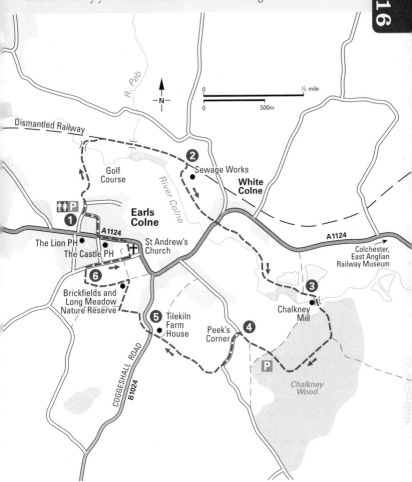

WALK 16 DIRECTIONS

❶ From the car park, turn left and left again into Burrows Road. Turn right, cross a road called Hillie Bunnies and keep ahead to climb a stile beside a public footpath sign and Wildside waymark. Follow the path downhill across the golf course, passing to the left of a pond, to reach a yellow waymark beside a footbridge. Cross this and bear left towards a hedge gap along a grassy path to join the railway nature reserve. Turn right on to the railway embankment and maintain direction keeping the river and golf course on your right. Cross the footbridge over the River Peb and maintain your direction for about 600yds (549m).

WALK 16

2 Leave the reserve by turning right at a collection of waymarks. Keep the fence of the sewage works on your left and follow the grassy path which later becomes a tarmac road, and pass through a kissing gate to reach Lower Holt Street. Turn left, cross the road, and follow the footpath and waymark between house Nos 20 and 22 through the wooden gate. Maintain direction across the meadow with the River Colne down on your right until you climb a stile.

left at the public footpath sign marked Park Lane. Follow the path through the kissing gate and turn immediately right along the path bounded by thick gorse bushes. Follow the path along the right-hand edge of woodland to a stile. Do not go over this but turn left beside a stream. Go through a kissing gate and walk along the field-edge path, keeping the hedgerow on your right, to an earth bridge where you turn right over the stream.

3 Turn right and cross the bridge over the Colne, passing kennels and Chalkney Mill on your right, and maintain direction into Chalkney Wood. Keep ahead at a crossing of paths and follow the track as it curves right to a parking area. Continue along the wide downhill track for 300yds (274m) and turn left into Tey Road at Peek's Corner.

6 Take the path past a Brickfields information board on your right and turn right at the top into Park Lane with St Andrews Church on your left. Turn left through the churchyard passing beside the lych gate to reach the High Street and return to the car park.

4 After 300yds (274m) turn right at the public footpath sign and go along the field-edge path keeping the hedgerows on your right. Cross the earth bridge through trees, maintain direction uphill, and pass Tilekiln Farm House, on your right, to Coggeshall Road.

5 Turn right at Coggeshall Road and as the road curves right turn

Six Farms and a Castle at Hedingham

Explore the wealth of history packed into this tiny area.

DISTANCE 3.5 miles (5.7km) **MINIMUM TIME** 1hr 30min

ASCENT/GRADIENT 64ft (20m) ▲▲▲ **LEVEL OF DIFFICULTY** ✦✦✦

PATHS Grassy, field-edge and farm tracks, some woodland and town streets

LANDSCAPE Arable and grazing farmland, patches of woodland

SUGGESTED MAP OS Explorer 195 Braintree & Saffron Walden

START / FINISH Grid reference: TL 784356

DOG FRIENDLINESS On lead round farms and on country lanes. Lots of other dogs around

PARKING Informal street parking in Castle Hedingham village

PUBLIC TOILETS Behind The Castle Hedingham Club in Church Lane

---

The Castle Hedingham story begins with Aubrey de Vere, a favourite knight of William the Conqueror, who was rewarded for his valour at the Battle of Hastings with land, which included Kensington and Earls Court in London. Aubrey's son built Castle Hedingham in 1140, which became the de Vere stronghold for the next 550 years and is still owned today by one of their descendants.

The de Veres became extremely rich and influential over the years and often entertained royalty, including Henry VIII and Elizabeth I. But they are best known for being great crusaders, fighting alongside Richard I (Richard the Lionheart) and taking leading parts in the famous battles at Crecy, Poitiers, Agincourt and Bosworth. Robert de Vere, 3rd Earl of Oxford, was one of the barons who persuaded King John to sign the Magna Carta at Runnymede in 1215.

But in 1703 the de Vere title fell out of use when Aubrey, 20th Earl of Oxford died, leaving no sons. The castle was purchased by Sir William Ashhurst, a Member of Parliament and Lord Mayor of London, who landscaped the grounds and built a fine country house, which was completed in 1719. The estate eventually passed to his great grandaughter, Elizabeth Houghton, who married Lewis Majendie. The Majendies owned Hedingham Estate for 250 years before it was inherited by a cousin who was descended from the de Veres.

A Star and Boar

This walk starts from the grand Norman Church of St Nicholas where, above the window of the Tudor bell tower, you can see the star and the boar, both symbols of the de Vere family. The star is said to have fallen from heaven upon the shield of the first de Vere on one of the crusades and since then has become the family emblem. The castle dominates the view as you walk along Castle Lane and uphill into open countryside dotted with farms, which date from the 16th and 17th centuries, and arable and grazing land.

Distinguished Drinkers

The tranquillity of the surrounding countryside is a far cry from the mayhem of the crusades and other famous battles. When you return to the village via a pleasant country lane, you cannot fail to notice the castle looming in the distance, a constant reminder of the power and influence of the de Vere dynasty. In the village, the tiny houses in Church Ponds cluster around the church, while those in Church Lane were the homes of weavers, built 400 years ago when the community benefited from the wool industry. Wander around and perhaps call in at the oldest pub, the Bell Inn, which dates back 500 years and is where Disraeli downed a pint or two after a speech. Or relax at the bar which, it is said, supported one or two de Veres too.

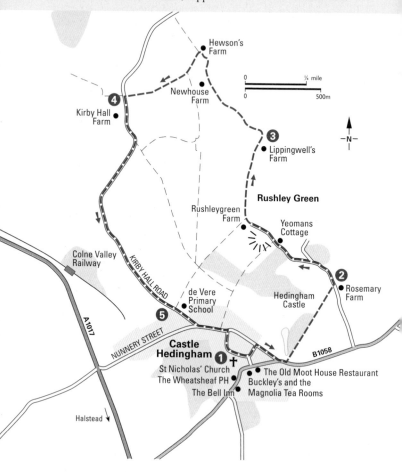

WALK 17 DIRECTIONS

❶ With the church on your right, walk along Church Ponds into Falcon Square with its medieval houses. Turn left into Castle Lane with the 17th-century former Youth Hostel building on your

right and walk uphill to Bayley Street. Cross the road and, at the castle entrance, turn right and walk to the T-junction. Turn left into Sudbury Road and, just after New Park Road on your right, turn left at the uphill narrow track to Rosemary Farm.

CASTLE HEDINGHAM

❷ Turn left, follow the track to the Y-junction and bear left passing the red-brick, thatched Keepers Cottage on your left. Pass several houses and admire the fine view of rolling countryside beyond the stile on your left, opposite Yeoman's cottage. After 200yds (183m) the track bears right with the converted barns of Rushleygreen Farm on your left. Ignore the timber footbridge immediately after the farm and continue along the main farm track with arable fields away to your left.

❸ Pass Lippingwell's Farm on your right and follow the meandering field-edge path passing the front of Newhouse Farm, with its pond on your left, and continue to Hewson's Farm

and the brick-built tower on your right. Turn sharp left at the public footpath sign along the field-edge path to the small row of trees at the rear of Newhouse Farm. At the waymark bear right across fields to Kirby Hall Farm.

❹ Turn left at the crossroads to Kirby Hall Road and, ignoring all footpaths left and right, follow this wide farm track passing hedgerows and rows of trees to return to Castle Hedingham. On the way, pass through high embankments of hedgerows and an impressive row of oak trees. Before rising towards the village of Hedingham you can see the top of the castle keep, peering above trees to your half left.

❺ Walking into the village, pass de Vere's Primary School and the modern housing estate on your left. At the T-junction, turn left into Nunnery Street and right into Crown Street, where jettied buildings and medieval cottages herald your return to the old village and the church.

Overleaf: Castle Hedingham

Halstead's Courtaulds Connection

A charming town and country walk discovering the influence of the Courtauld family and their textile legacy.

DISTANCE *3 miles (4.8km)* **MINIMUM TIME** *1hr 15min*

ASCENT/GRADIENT *90ft (27m)* ▲▲▲ **LEVEL OF DIFFICULTY** +++

PATHS *Town streets and grassy tracks*

LANDSCAPE *Urban, river and meadow*

SUGGESTED MAP *OS Explorer 195 Braintree & Saffron Walden*

START / FINISH *Grid reference: TL 812306*

DOG FRIENDLINESS *Pleasant on-lead town walk but most dogs will prefer the meadow*

PARKING *Pay-and-display in Chapel Street*

PUBLIC TOILETS *Chapel Street*

Surrounded by the gentle rolling countryside of the Colne Valley in north Essex, Halstead developed over many centuries as a busy market town and, in the Middle Ages, much of its prosperity came from the wool trade. In the early 19th century Samuel Courtauld (1793–1881), an industrious and successful businessman, brought a new lease of life to the town. A descendant of a Huguenot refugee family, he set up in business as a silk throwster (a person who twists silk fibres into thread) and his family went on to found the internationally known Courtaulds company.

A Royal Trendsetter

Courtaulds had its share of ups and downs, but always seemed one step ahead of its competitors, due to a policy of diversification. When the silk industry dwindled, mainly due to French competition, the company specialised in the production of mourning crêpe, which was to become the definitive fashion material during, and after, Queen Victoria's reign (1837–1901). When crêpe fell out of favour, Courtaulds turned to the manufacture of artificial silk which became such a success that brand name materials such as Celanese saw the company through the depression of the 1930s.

The Courtaulds connection with Halstead began in 1825 when Samuel Courtauld bought the present Townsford Mill and converted it to produce silk-woven fabrics; much of the raw material was imported in bulk from India. In those days the cloth was produced in the workers' homes and some of these early weavers' cottages can still be seen next to the mill in Bridge Street. By 1891 the mill became one of England's largest employers, where 1,400 people, the vast majority young girls and women, toiled at 1,000 looms.

The Courtauld family left legacies throughout Halstead and on this walk you will discover some of them, such as the Jubilee Fountain at the top of Market Street, on a spot previously occupied by the old Market Cross. In Hedingham Lane you can see the Courtaulds workers' houses which are named after characters and titles from Jane Austen's novels. The family also footed the bill for building Halstead Cottage Hospital while the Homes of Rest next door, a semi-circular row of single-storey dwellings built in 1923, provided much-needed housing for retired silk weavers.

Courtauld Institute

Samuel Courtauld became very rich, and lived to the ripe old age of 88 in an impressive Tudor mansion called Gosfield Hall, a few miles from Halstead. During the 1920s his great-nephew and namesake would often drive or walk along Box Mill where he apparently took a dislike to the housing and duly replaced them with his own preferred style of cottages. The young Samuel (1876–1947) went on to establish the Courtauld Institute of Art in London before he died. In 1982 Courtaulds factory finally closed down but there's little doubt that this name lives on in Halstead.

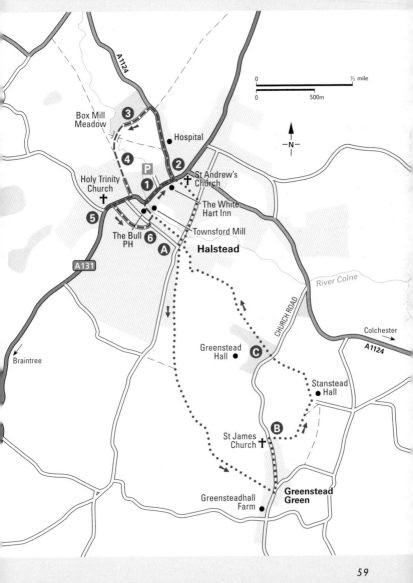

WALK 18 DIRECTIONS

❶ Turn right into Chapel Street then left into the High Street by the former post office. Walk up Market Hill to the Jubilee Drinking Fountain for panoramic views of the layout of the town and note the undulating landscape, proof that not all of Essex is flat.

WHAT TO LOOK OUT FOR

Three-storey weavers' homes were still fairly common in Halstead during the 19th and early 20th centuries. Some of these survive in Weavers Row near Parsonage Street.

❷ Turn left into Hedingham Road (A1124) passing Halstead Hospital and the Courtauld Homes of Rest on your right. Turn left into Box Mill Lane where several cottages and larger dwellings attest to further building by the Courtaulds.

❸ At the end of Box Mill Lane, maintain direction into Box Mill Meadow, a fine picnic spot, and cross the footbridge over the River Colne as it flows south into the town. Two mills, a watermill and a wind-powered one, once occupied this spot. Take the footpath to the left, which later veers away from the river.

❹ At the edge of Halstead Town Football Ground, cross the stile

WHILE YOU'RE THERE

Some of the oldest houses in Halstead, dating back to the 14th century, can be seen at the bottom of Chapel Hill. At the top of the High Street is the flint and rubble St Andrew's Church with its lovely tower; some parts date back to the 15th century.

and maintain your direction along the footpath which becomes a grassy track, the former route of the Halstead and Colne Valley Railway. Go straight ahead into Butler Road, which was named after R A Butler (1902–82), better known as Rab, Conservative politician and Member of Parliament for Saffron Walden. At the T-junction with Trinity Street notice the redevelopment across the road, where flats and a park area behind them now stand on the site of the old railway station.

❺ Turn right, past an alley called Rail Yard, and walk to Trinity Church on your right. Close by are some of the oldest houses in the town. Retrace your steps for a few paces and turn right just after the police station into New Street. Note the public gardens opposite the Methodist church, turn left into Martins Road, then left again and right into Factory Lane West.

❻ Continue ahead and turn left into The Causeway. Courtaulds old Townsford Mill is on the right, and walk ahead into Bridge Street. To the left is Halstead Library, built in 1865. Turn right to cross the bridge over the River Colne and go into the High Street to the former post office. Pause here awhile to note the varied architecture around you. Walk along Chapel Street and return to the car park.

WHERE TO EAT AND DRINK

You are spoiled for choice with tea rooms, restaurants and pubs. Of particular historic interest are two 500-year-old coaching inns in the High Street: The White Hart, which ran a regular service to Great Yarmouth, and The Bull, which featured in the TV series *Lovejoy*.

To Greenstead Green

*A longer loop walk which takes in a pretty church
and rural calm.*

See map and information panel for Walk 18

DISTANCE 7.75 miles (12.5km)   **MINIMUM TIME** 2hrs 30min
ASCENT/GRADIENT 154ft (47m) ▲▲▲   **LEVEL OF DIFFICULTY** ✦✦✦

WALK 19 DIRECTIONS
(Walk 18 option)

To extend the walk to Greenstead Green turn right, Point **A**, into Factory Lane West, which passes Townsford Mill and continues to the right. At the T-junction turn right into Parsonage Street, cross the roundabout and take the footpath to the left of Tiding Hill, passing behind houses to cross Highfields into South Close.

Between Nos 20 and 22, take the path towards the meadow and bear right along the field-edge path (south). Maintain your direction across the earth bridge and after 500yds (457m) you will pass a fingerpost on the field-edge path. Continue downhill and pass through a hedge gap following the winding track to Church Road. Turn left at Greensteadhall Farm and pass cottages before reaching St James Church, Point **B**.

Greenstead Green owes much of its ecclesiastical heritage to Mary Gee. Born in 1795 she married into an influential Essex family and later became a wealthy widow. She bore the cost of constructing St James' Church in 1844, the vicarage and the school, as well as Halstead's Holy Trinity Church.

In St James' look at the north wall which has two plaques, one dedicated to Mary Gee, the other to an American airman whose plane crashed near by in World War Two.

Cross Church Road to the public footpath sign opposite the vicarage, and take the field-edge path for 250yds (229m) keeping the hedgerow on your right. Turn left, still with the hedgerow on your right, and maintain direction passing Stanstead Hall. As you pass a series of paddocks keep to the diverted footpath. Turn left, keeping hedgerows to your left, and follow the path down to Church Road, Point **C**.

Pass the Lodge on your right, climb the stile and take the cross-field path diagonally through the meadow. On your left, through trees, is Greenstead Hall. Climb the next stile and follow the cross-field path diagonally downhill keeping the spire of St Andrew's Church in view in the distance. Follow the path towards the rear of houses on your left to join with Cooks Close. Take the enclosed footpath ahead and turn right downhill into Ball's Chase, then, at the roundabout, right again into Parsonage Street. Continue uphill to the High Street by St Andrew's Church, turn left and return to the car park.

Overleaf: The view across Box Hill Meadow at Halstead

Braintree and the Flitch Way

Braintree's industrial heritage and a stroll along a disused railway line.

DISTANCE 5.5 miles (8.8km)   **MINIMUM TIME** 2hrs 15min

ASCENT/GRADIENT 48ft (15m) ▲▲▲   **LEVEL OF DIFFICULTY** ✚✚✚

PATHS Grassy and gravel tracks, some street walking

LANDSCAPE Wildlife-rich railway cuttings, river bank and urban landscape

SUGGESTED MAP OS Explorer 195 Braintree & Saffron Walden

START / FINISH Grid reference: TL 760227

DOG FRIENDLINESS Pedestrians and dogs share Flitch Way with cyclists and horses so may have to be on lead

PARKING Pay-and-display car parks at George Yard, Manor Street (behind the library) and Braintree Station

PUBLIC TOILETS Ground floor of George Yard car park and Braintree Station

---

WALK 20 DIRECTIONS

The attractive town sits astride the junction of two Roman roads, where The White Hart Hotel, a former coaching and posting house, now stands. In the 19th century, Samuel Courtauld, a descendant of a Huguenot weaving family, created a successful textile industry in the town. Further prosperity was brought by iron foundries and manufacturing businesses including the window-making enterprise set up by Francis Crittall who started as an ironmonger in the late 19th century. He became one of the town's major employers, producing metal-framed windows, the forerunner of double glazing.

In this walk you will discover Courtaulds' and Crittall's contributions to the town and see how Braintree is facing the future with a regeneration programme. Yet for all the changes, the town still retains links with the past with an interesting heritage trail and a linear country park, the Flitch Way, following the railway line, from Braintree to Bishop's Stortford, abandoned in 1969.

The walk starts from Braintree Station where a set of buffers terminates the old line from Liverpool Street in London to Bishop's Stortford. Beyond is the Flitch Way, a tarmac trail approached via the path at the western end of the station car park by a Flitch Way Country Park sign. The path soon crosses the bridge over Notley Road.

After a mile (1.6 km) the path crosses the bridge over the A1256, shortly followed a fingerpost at a crossing of paths. Turn right and follow the waymarked path through a housing estate. Cross a footbridge, later bearing right as indicated by the waymark and then keep ahead through trees and another housing estate. Keep the river on your right until you reach Clap Bridge on Rayne Road, the former Roman road of Stane Street. Turn right across the bridge, continue over the roundabout and into the town to The White Hart Hotel. Pass to the right of the hotel into Coggeshall Road and keep ahead to the double roundabout. Cross Railway Street and, on your right, there is a block of apartments fronted by a heritage board describing the site of the Crittalls Manor Works, demolished in 1992. Continue along Coggeshall Road looking out on your left for John Ray Street, where a pair of weathered timber gates mark the entrance to the recreation ground, a gift to the town from Julian Courtauld.

Back in Coggeshall Road, turn right into Cressing Road to The Kings Head pub, opposite which a great oak tree once grew. In 1964 the tree was removed because it was considered too big and dangerous, but many townspeople remember sitting on the bench beneath it to watch the world go by. In Cressing Road there is an interesting mix of late 19th-century cottages, and an impressive thatched cottage dating from 1620.

WHILE YOU'RE THERE

Visit the spectacular aisled barns at nearby Cressing Temple, built 800 years ago by the Knights Templar. The Wheat Barn has an exhibition explaining the history of this elite force. If you're there on a Sunday join the free guided tour or wander round the Tudor walled garden.

At the end of Cressing Road cross over to Clockhouse Way, a conservation area of houses constructed with concrete blocks, complete with Crittall metal windows. Built for Crittall workers in 1918–19, the design

WHERE TO EAT AND DRINK

There are plenty of pubs in Braintree including The White Hart Hotel opposite Rayne Road (Roman Stane Street), which serves excellent bar snacks and wholesome lunches in an atmospheric setting and The Swan in Bank Street. Eatons in George Yard has tasty snacks and outdoor seating.

was copied, in 1926, at Silver End (to the south-east of Braintree).

Return to the junction and continue down Chapel Hill. At the end, turn half left to the roundabout then turn right on to Mill Hill. Go under the railway bridge, on the left is another heritage board describing the site of an old flour mill which Courtauld converted into a silk mill, and which is now a residential area.

Turn right up Skitts Hill, go under the railway bridge and take the first right into The Yard, a modern complex of apartments. Keep left and follow the footpath towards the gas works where a heritage board describes the function of Lake and Elliot's Power House, which generated electricity for use by the town's businesses until 1946 when the National Grid started lighting up the country. The firm originally produced cycle parts then expanded into jacks and armour plating for the military. Like other businesses they no longer operate in town, but they have been replaced by new initiatives keeping Braintree the bustling town it has always been. Follow the footpath into Manor Street, turn left passing modern developments in Trinovantian Way and return to your car park.

Langdon – an Old Plot for Eastenders

Explore ancient woodland and grassy meadows where Eastenders fulfilled a dream of living in a house in the country.

DISTANCE 3.75 miles (6km) **MINIMUM TIME** 1hr 30min

ASCENT/GRADIENT 230ft (70m) ▲▲▲ **LEVEL OF DIFFICULTY** +++

PATHS Forest, field and horse tracks

LANDSCAPE Woodland, meadows, ponds, farmland and ruins of urban housing developments

SUGGESTED MAP OS Explorer 175 Southend-on-Sea & Basildon

START / FINISH Grid reference: TQ 659873

DOG FRIENDLINESS Great forest and field romp with plenty of other dogs; bowl of water outside Visitor Centre

PARKING Free parking at Langdon Visitor Centre, Lower Dunton Road

PUBLIC TOILETS Langdon Visitor Centre

Langdon Nature Reserve is an example of how abandoned urbanisations can become a haven for wildlife. Much of the area, now managed by Essex Wildlife Trust, was formerly known as Plotlands. But where did this strange name come from? Back in the 1890s, a great agricultural depression ravaged the farming communities of Essex. The farmlands, around what is now the urban fringes of Basildon, were taken out of production and became redundant. They were divided into small plots and sold to Eastenders from London who dreamed of a self-sufficient lifestyle in the country.

The Good Life

Between the turn of the century and 1940, these 'Plotlanders', as they became known, built hundreds of modest chalets and bungalows as weekend retreats or holiday homes. Many families would travel up from London by train carrying building materials with them. They lived in makeshift bell tents while the man of the house went about the DIY.

Permanent residency was forbidden at Langdon because there was no proper sanitation or other services. For many Plotlanders, it was a bucket in the back and an old gas lamp to light the way if they needed the loo. But rural Essex was still a relatively quiet backwater, and most residents seemed happy to forego some modern conveniences in return for an escape from the bustle and overcrowding of the East End. At the outbreak of World War Two the authorities turned a blind eye as many Eastenders moved to Langdon to escape the horror of the Blitz and survived by growing their own fruit and vegetables. But in 1949 the Plotlands at Langdon were compulsorily purchased and demolished to make way for Basildon New Town. In this walk you can see what's left of these idealistic dwellings, with their overgrown gardens and orchards which, nearly half a century later, support a rich mixture of wild flowers and animals.

With 460 acres (186ha) of meadows, woods, ponds, plantation and scrub, Langdon is Essex Wildlife Trust's largest inland reserve. What makes

LANGDON

Langdon so unusual, is not so much the rarity of its plant and animal life, but the many species — once commonplace in the countryside and now threatened by intensive farming and development — which thrive here. You may be lucky enough to spot badgers, foxes and weasels not to mention hundreds of orchids, butterflies and flowering plants. In the former Plotland ruins and gardens you'll even find adders and lizards.

Ancient Woodlands

In 1969, when plans were discovered that the meadows were to be turned into a housing development, there was public outcry and the idea was thankfully shelved. Today, the large grassy areas of Willow Park are still traditionally managed by grazing and haycutting and, in summer, wild flowers attract butterflies and insects. In spring the ancient woodlands of Marks Hill, Lincewood and Longwood are carpeted with primroses, wood anemones and bluebells, helped along by rotational coppicing, another form of ancient woodland management, which enables plants and animals to thrive. In your tramp through these ancient woodlands you'll not only discover ponds filled with great crested frogs and toads, but, as Langdon Hills is the highest point in Essex, you'll be privy to some of the most far-reaching panoramas of London.

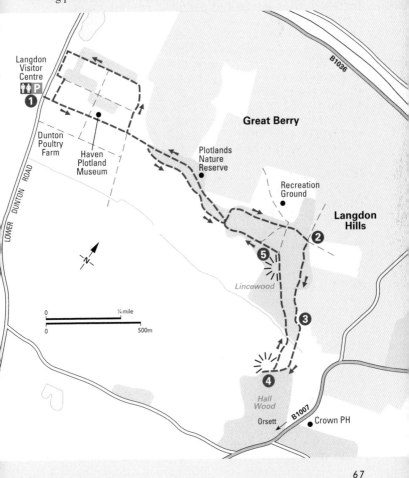

WALK 21 DIRECTIONS

❶ From the car park, walk up the straight wide avenue of Plotlands signposted 'Plotlands Walk', passing the museum on your left. At a crossing of paths by red waymark No 1, keep ahead through the woodland path, with fields on your right, and occasional views of south Essex between the trees. Ignoring other paths, continue along this bridle path and at the metal fence look left for the recreation ground. Continue along the path for 100yds (91m) until you reach wide cross paths.

❷ Turn right at red waymark No 2. You are now in Lincewood. The path undulates through high trees and open woodland, passing behind houses on your left, and red waymark No 3.

❸ Ignore a set of steps by a red and white marker on your left and at waymark No 4 beside four steep wooden steps, then turn right along the path, keeping the wooden fencing enclosing Hall Wood on your left. Walk for 20yds (18m), to a break in the trees and go over a stile for views of the London skyline. Retrace your steps and take the first path on your left downhill, towards the wooden barrier, beside a Nature Reserve sign.

❹ Follow this narrow track downhill through ferns, and after 200yds (183m) reach the duckboard skirting the pond.

Note the large oak tree growing from the banks of the pond forming a low arch across the duckboard. Continue ahead through the kissing gate and walk downhill as the path meanders and undulates through open woodland, with ferns and patches of meadow awash with bluebells in spring. Continue along this path to the wooden bench beneath the large oak tree, where there are superb views of rolling farmland and London in the distance.

❺ A further 50yds (46m) ahead, at the Y-junction, take the left-hand path downhill keeping the arable field on your left. Go through the pair of timber posts and turn left on to the wide grassy bridleway. After a footbridge beside a barrier turn right and after 20yds (18m) turn left on to another grassy path. Pass beside a wooden gate and maintain direction through two meadows, keeping the houses on your right. At the end of the second meadow pass beside a barrier, turn right and ahead is red waymark No 1. Here, turn right keeping the Plotland ruins on your left. Pass the Plotland Trail waymarks 5 and 6, turn left at the next bridle path and follow the waymarks back to the car park.

Wandering in Weald Country Park

A fairly strenuous walk taking in the history of a
great Tudor mansion and a royal deer park.

DISTANCE 5 miles (8km)   **MINIMUM TIME** 2hrs 15min

ASCENT/GRADIENT 117ft (35m) ▲▲▲   **LEVEL OF DIFFICULTY** ✦✦✦

PATHS Open parkland, forest tracks and some cross-field footpaths

LANDSCAPE Undulating deer parkland, ponds, lakes and mixed woodland

SUGGESTED MAP OS Explorer 175 Southend-on-Sea & Basildon

START / FINISH Grid reference: TQ 568941

DOG FRIENDLINESS Wonderful open spaces for a romp but watch out for grazing cattle and ducks

PARKING Free car parks at Visitor Centre, Belvedere and Cricket Green on Weald Road and Lincolns Lane

PUBLIC TOILETS Visitor Centre and inside park

Weald Country Park's origins are back in 1062 when the land was a gift from King Harold to the Abbots of Waltham. The abbots managed the land (which was worked by peasants), added fallow deer which they hunted, and over the years the estate prospered. All this came to an end when Henry VIII dissolved the monasteries and stripped them of their lands and goods. Weald was passed to the King's closest allies.

Discover a Country Park

In this walk you will discover a mixture of formal landscapes, with lakes and woodlands, and spot fallow deer – elements which make this country park one of the finest in Essex. You will also take a trip into history as you explore the site of Weald Hall, a fine Tudor mansion, built in 1540 and extended over the years by various owners. In Tudor times owning a deer park brought more prestige than having your own moat, but less than having your own private gallows.

A Multitude of Owners

By 1800 the mansion had 40 bedrooms and provided jobs and housing for around 50 people. The first owner was Sir Brian Tuke, Henry VIII's treasurer, who was followed by a succession of nouveau riche individuals who made their money by trade or in government. One of these, Sir Anthony Browne, a judge, politician and favourite of Mary I, and who lived here in 1550, went on to become the founder of Brentwood School and provided almhouses for the poor. Although knighted by Queen Elizabeth, he persecuted Protestants during Mary's reign and was responsible for the death of a young apprentice, William Hunter, who was burned at the stake in Brentwood. A memorial to Hunter stands in the town.

But easily the most tyrannous of owners was William Scroggs, Lord Chief Justice to Charles II in 1678. He sent over 20 men to the gallows, and was so detested that when he died all traces of him were removed,

WEALD COUNTRY PARK

including his face from a portrait at the top of the stairs in Weald Hall. In 1756, the Towers, a family of lawyers, bought the estate and owned it for the next 200 years. During World War Two over 30,000 troops were stationed at Weald. Sadly Weald Hall fell into disrepair and the deer escaped, but in 1987 they were replaced. The house was demolished in the 1950s, but you can go to the top of Belvedere Hill where there are wonderful views over the parkland and you can get a real sense of the extent and grandeur of this royal hunting estate hundreds of years ago.

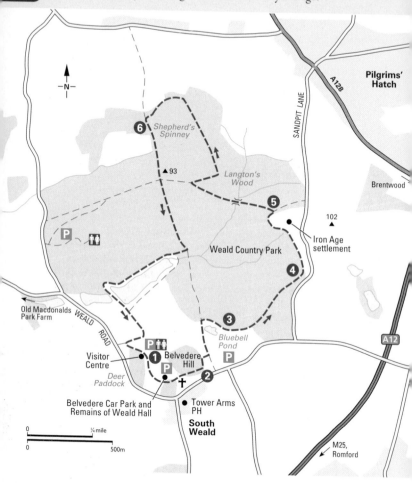

WALK 22 DIRECTIONS

❶ With your back to Weald Road, turn right out of the car park past a fingerpost beside the parks office hut. Keep the red-brick wall on your right and continue to the Belvedere car park – the site of the foundations of Weald Hall. On your left are the

WEALD COUNTRY PARK

remains of steps leading up to part of the original building. Walk into the car park and take the earth path uphill between trees. Bear left, keeping the church on your right, and pass the door which used to give access to the graves of the Tower family. At the end of the church wall, turn left through trees and go on to the grassy knoll. This overlooks the original gardens of the estate and the site of Weald Hall.

❷ Keeping the gardens to your left, walk up the steps to the site of Belvedere Hill where there is an information board. Spectators would watch hunting and indulge in banquets. Walk down the steps, turn right and take the path downhill, between conifers, to open parkland. Maintain direction and go through a gate on your right and continue, keeping Bluebell Pond and the cricket field on your right.

❸ Follow the grassy path uphill, passing the bridleway waymarks on your right. At the top of the hill, pass through a thickly wooded area of ancient hornbeam and silver birch, and continue along the bridleway, which runs parallel with Sandpit Lane.

❹ As the path veers away from the road, note the steep embankment to your right – the remains of an Iron Age settlement.

You are now walking around what was the moat. Keep to the path through meadow and parkland and, at the tree-clad embankment rising to your right, continue clockwise until you join the hard track.

❺ Turn left through the tree gap to walk downhill beside a fence. Pass to the left of a house. cross a footbridge and keep ahead through the wood. Go through a kissing gate on the right and turn right along a wide, grassy path. At a path junction turn right by a red and white post and turn left at a yellow waymarked post. Turn left just after a barrier and follow the bridleway that borders Shepherd's Spinney.

❻ At the next crossing of paths by a barrier keep ahead, passing to the left of grassland. After 800yds (732m) turn right before the kissing gate to walk with the lake on your left. At the end of the lake, turn left over the footbridge and return to the car park passing the deer paddock.

WALK 23

Two Halls in Thorndon Country Park

A close encounter with Thorndon Hall and the ruins of Old Hall amid woodland paths and views of the Thames Estuary.

DISTANCE 4.5 miles (7 km)   MINIMUM TIME 2hrs

ASCENT/GRADIENT Negligible ▲▲▲   LEVEL OF DIFFICULTY +++

PATHS Track and field paths

LANDSCAPE Mainly field and woodland paths with views across countryside to the Thames Estuary

SUGGESTED MAP OS Explorer 175 Southend-on-Sea & Basildon

START / FINISH Grid reference: TQ 608915

DOG FRIENDLINESS Keep on a lead though grazing areas

PARKING Thorndon North Country Park (pay-and-display)

PUBLIC TOILETS By the Countryside Centre

The 500-acre (200ha) Thorndon Country Park is one of Essex Wildlife Trust's most popular centres. It also attracts huge numbers of woodland birds and a variety of butterflies, including some rare species. The Countryside Centre was built from trees blown over during the 1987 storms and the park itself comprises ancient woodland and ponds and parkland landscaped by Capability Brown in the 18th century. Traditional farming techniques have been restored on some of the land grazed by rare breeds including English White Cattle.

Near to the start of the walk is an ancient deer park dating from the 15th century which is now a designated Site of Special Scientific Interest (SSSI) and one of the most important habitats in the park.

Old and New Halls

The site of Old Hall, the original mansion built in the grounds dates from the Domesday Book of 1086 but a fire destroyed the house in the early 1700s. However, the magnificent portico, imported from Italy, was saved and assembled in the new mansion, Thorndon Hall, when it was rebuilt nearby in the 1760s. The owner Lord Petre was a talented botanist and gardener whose hothouses were said to be the largest in the world.

Around 100 years later this mansion was also burned down and it remained in ruins until 1976 when developers rebuilt it and sympathetically converted it into the luxury apartments we see today.

The walk passes both of these sites and Old Hall is particularly beguiling, as the area where it lay has been transformed into a wildlife haven. Although excavations were carried out in the 1950s the results were disappointing and only the remains of broken wine bottles, pottery and fragments of Delft wall tiles were found. Today, the invading woodland is all that remains of Old Hall.

THORNDON COUNTRY PARK

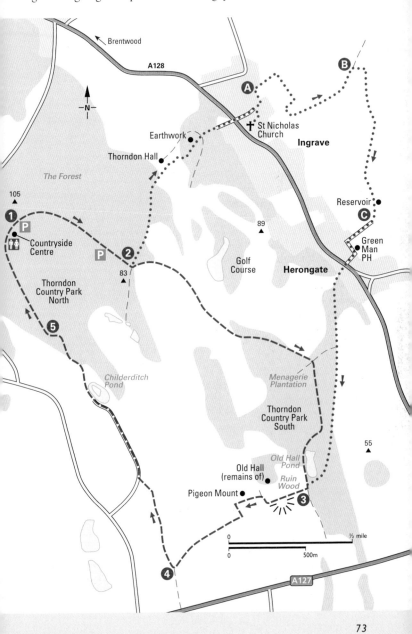

WALK 23 DIRECTIONS

❶ With your back to the Countryside Centre turn right along a path through woods signposted 'Woodland Trail' to pass red waymark No 1. Turn right through a gate to pass

waymark No 2 and then turn left, go through a gate and across a car park to reach a track and keep ahead.

❷ Go through a gate, cross the track and take the path ahead, signposted The Woodland Trust.

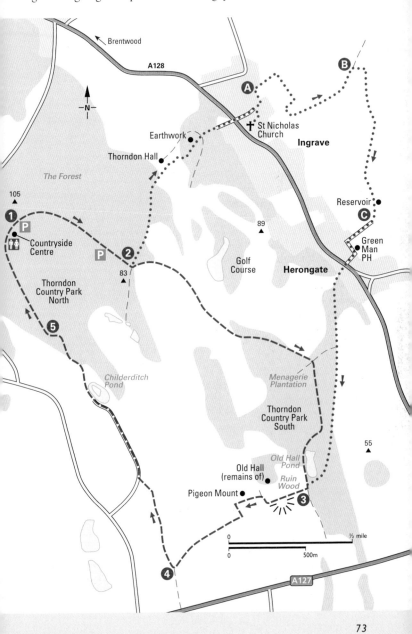

WHAT TO LOOK OUT FOR

The house at No 21 just before the Green Man was once the village butcher's shop. Notice the sloping tiled roof and the original shop windows. The nearby slaughterhouse, now a pine show room, dates from the 17th century.

Keep ahead for about 1 mile and at the T-junction, enter Menagerie Plantation through the gate ahead and follow the waymarked Wildside Walk. Look out for where you cross a boardwalk on the right and continue to the right of Old Hall Pond.

3 Turn right at the junction, go through a kissing gate and bear left along the field edge path. To the left are views towards the North Downs and on your right is Ruin Wood, with the remains of Old Hall, and now a wildlife haven. Go through the gate and bear left to pass through a hedge gap. In the corner of the field turn left through a kissing-gate, then bear right and head downhill to a waymarked post and go through a gate.

4 Turn right, enter a field via a gate and bear left across it to cross a plank footbridge. At a track turn left and almost immediately cross a stile on the right. Head diagonally across a field, cross another stile and turn right along a lane which becomes a track. After passing Childerditch Pond go through a gate into a meadow. Follow the red waymarks along the lower right-hand edge of the meadow and in the corner, go through a gate and then cross a footbridge to a crossroads.

5 Continue uphill through woodland, turn left at the T-junction and follow the track as it curves right, and back to the start of the walk.

WHERE TO EAT AND DRINK

The Green Man is an attractive looking pub with a garden just opposite the village green but a few yards further, just off the walking route, is the Olde Dog Inn, a 16th century weather boarded inn which is well worth the short detour. This Free House offers a good selection of real ales and is great on atmosphere. The composer Vaughan Williams used to drink here on his visits.

WHILE YOU'RE THERE

Stop by the information board after the site of the Old Hall from where you will see ahead of you a large mound. This is called Pigeon Mount and was once the site of an octagonal tower that had a spiral path leading to a door at the top. The views over the Thames Estuary from there must have been spectacular.

And on to Ingrave and Herongate

Where Vaughan Williams and William Byrd found inspiration.
See map and information panel for Walk 23

DISTANCE 3.5 miles (5.6km)   **MINIMUM TIME** 1hr 30min
ASCENT/GRADIENT Negligible ▲▲▲   **LEVEL OF DIFFICULTY** ✦✦✦

WALK 24 DIRECTIONS
(Walk 23 option)

After passing The Woodland Trust signpost after Point ❷, turn next left in the direction of Ingrave. Keep ahead with Thorndon Park Golf Course on your right and soon the path passes beside Thorndon Hall, built when the original hall was burnt down. In 1976 the mansion was converted into luxury apartments.

Keep ahead, cross a footbridge and shortly you will pass to the right of an earthwork before reaching the access road to Thorndon Hall. Cross this and pass houses to reach the A128.

Cross the road and continue along St Nicholas Grove, turn right into Salmonds Grove and right at the public footpath sign to visit St Nicholas church. Built by Lord Petre, many locals thought it resembled a water tower. Retrace your steps and where St Nicholas Grove ends follow the tarmac path beside houses and turn right to cross a stile at the next public footpath sign, Point Ⓐ.

The composer Vaughan Williams frequently visited Ingrave and the nearby villages and was so taken with the local folk songs that he collected more than 100 of them and went on to use 35 of

these tunes for hymns. Another great composer of church music, William Byrd, had also found inspiration here back in the 16th century and often visited Thorndon Hall.

Once over a boardwalk turn right and continue ahead to where the field ends beside a band of woodland. Here turn right along the footpath, then make two left turns and keep ahead along the right-hand field edge to a hedge gap, Point Ⓑ.

Turn right here and after 50yds (45m) turn right through the metal barrier to walk along the right-hand edge of the next field. Cross a plank footbridge and keep ahead. Bear right through a hedge gap and keep to the right of the metal fence to the reservoir, to a tarmac road, Point Ⓒ.

Turn right and at the end turn left and at the Green Man pub turn right to cross the A128 and enter the wood to your right, by a public footpath sign. At the set of public footpath signs go through the gate ahead and soon you will see the lowland of Thorndon Park South to your right, shortly followed by Old Hall Pond. At the crossing of paths turn right to pass to the left of the pond and go through the kissing gate to rejoin walk 23 at Point ❸.

DAVY DOWN

Dipping into Davy Down

Combine wonderful woodland walking and riverside views with a visit to one of the south-east's busiest shopping centres.

DISTANCE 4 miles (6.4km)	**MINIMUM TIME** 1hr 30min

ASCENT/GRADIENT 50ft (15m) ▲▲▲ **LEVEL OF DIFFICULTY** ✦✦✦

PATHS Forest tracks, river bank and grassy paths prone to muddiness, boardwalk

LANDSCAPE Meadow, woodland, flood plains and river

SUGGESTED MAP OS Explorer 162 Greenwich & Gravesend

START / FINISH Grid reference: TQ 594798

DOG FRIENDLINESS Good place for a romp off-lead in woods

PARKING Free car parks at Davy Down and Stifford Bridge

PUBLIC TOILETS Davy Down Visitors' Centre

WALK 25 DIRECTIONS

Davy Down is part of the Thames Chase Community Forest, one of 12 such forests in England covering large areas close to towns and cities. Far from being continuous plantings of trees in the traditional sense, community forests are a conglomeration of wooded landscapes which may include farmland, villages, nature areas and public open spaces. The aim of the community forest is to create easily accessible landscapes for wildlife, work, education and recreation.

Davy Down nestles in the Mardyke Valley, among large modern developments to the north-east of Lakeside Shopping Centre. Once used for market gardening, the land was taken over in 1985 as part of the Thames Chase Community Forest when the A13 trunk road was built, thus bringing to an end a long history of farming. The derelict outbuildings were replaced by the Davy Down visitors' car park. From this abandoned farmland, new landscapes are being created – you will see ponds and wetlands, new woodland hedgerows and areas planted with more than 4,000 trees.

Start from the visitors' car park, where you can still see remnants of the old farm's gate posts and garden plants. Go through the gate and follow the path as it winds its way through the site, passing the Stifford Pumping Station which still extracts water from the 150ft (46m) bore hole in the chalk below. After climbing earth steps towards the pumping station, walk to the left towards trees and on to the boardwalk which bisects three ponds.

WHILE YOU'RE THERE

Lakeside Shopping Centre is west of Davy Down. This centre attracts millions of shoppers each year and contains more than 300 shops, a food court, a multiplex cinema and a watersports complex.

76

DAVY DOWN

In the distance the 1892 railway viaduct spans the valley. Below is a small modern footbridge which you cross to link up with the Mardyke Way. The River Mardyke winds its way through the Plain of Thurrock, from its source, 8 miles (12.9km) upstream, to the River Thames at Purfleet, meandering through Davy Down where the valley is dominated by flood plain meadows bounded by ancient woodlands.

Until the 15th century the valley was mainly wet fenland, much like the rest of Essex. The land was drained for agriculture and the course of the river was straightened. Work has begun to increase access in the valley and to improve the landscape and wildlife habitat. This will include efforts to return the channelled river to a more natural feature, by creating shelves and bays and planting trees and hedgerows.

Cross the footbridge, turn left, follow the path round a sharp right bend and take the first path right into Brannetts Wood, one of the oldest recorded ancient woodlands in south Essex. The track, through thick foliage and tall trees, rises gently and soon bears left in a westerly direction. After 0.5 mile (800m), a cross path indicates the start of the less dense Millards Green ahead. Turn left here and, after 30yds (27m), rejoin the grassy Mardyke Way cross path keeping the fence on your right.

Beyond the fence the meadow flood plain stretches to the Mardyke River which, in summer, is accessible on foot, but soon floods after heavy rains. Retrace your steps beneath the viaduct along the wide grassy riverside path. Ignore

WHAT TO LOOK OUT FOR

Water voles love wet areas such as rivers, ditches and ponds and there's no shortage of these at Davy Down. Loss of suitable habitat through urban development, increased river bank mowing, dredging and degradation of river banks spell danger for these small creatures – now a protected species.

the modern footbridge and continue over the next bridge, Stifford Bridge, where medieval pilgrims once crossed on their way to Canterbury. Turn right and walk towards the viaduct in the distance. This riverside path has occasional seating overlooking the water where you can watch damselflies in the summer months. Look out too, for glow worms.

Just before the viaduct the path forks. Follow the right-hand path and, after 200yds (183m), take the path right, uphill, and walk between rows of native tree saplings, part of a new woodland scheme. The path continues uphill and passes quite close to the Stifford road. Looking left, there is a marvellous view of Davy Down and the pumping station. Follow the path back to the car park.

WHERE TO EAT AND DRINK

There are no places to stop for refreshments on this walk but, if you're driving, try the Dog and Partridge pub at Stifford (no food 3pm–6pm, Monday–Friday), or the Royal Oak (food served all day) at South Ockendon overlooking The Green. Both are dog- and child-friendly establishments. Otherwise, head for Lakeside where there are dozens of eateries to choose from.

Willingale – a Pint-sized Parish with Two Churches

*An easy stroll along the Essex Way which includes
one of the county's most rural villages.*

DISTANCE 3.75 miles (6km) **MINIMUM TIME** 1hr 30min

ASCENT/GRADIENT 33ft (11m) ▲▲▲ **LEVEL OF DIFFICULTY** ✦✦✦

PATHS Field-edge paths, riverside meadows and green lane

LANDSCAPE Rolling countryside, arable farmland and river

SUGGESTED MAP OS Explorer 183 Chelmsford & The Rodings,
Maldon & Witham

START / FINISH Grid reference: TL 597076

DOG FRIENDLINESS Should be on lead for most of walk

PARKING Free car park at Willingale Village Hall

PUBLIC TOILETS None en route

So tiny is the peaceful and picturesque village of Willingale in central Essex, that if you blink you'll miss it. Its cottages and houses are spread out over quite a large area, and the focal point of the village, its two churches – St Andrew's and St Christopher's – are unique in Essex as they share the same churchyard.

Sibling Rivalry

All sorts of myths abound as to how this came about, but a story, which has now become part of village folklore, tells of an argument between two sisters which resulted in each deciding to build her own church. It's a story that may keep the passing visitor entertained, but since St Christopher's was built 200 years after St Andrew's, one of the quarrelling sisters must have discovered the key to longevity. What they argued about nobody really knows, but maybe their differences were down to that age-old problem concerning women – men.

Additional Spiritual Care

Perhaps we shall never know the real cause of their rivalry, but a more likely explanation for the churches, is in the names of the two parishes, Willingale Spain and Willingale Doe. In the 12th century Hervey d'Espania built Spains Hall and the church in Willingale Spain and also gave his name to the parish. Then in the 14th century, at a time when the wool industry was expanding, the d'Ou family settled in Willingale. Workers were attracted to the area and St Andrew's simply couldn't cope with the population explosion. The d'Ou family built St Christopher's Church on the site of the already consecrated land and this is probably where the name Willingale Doe originates.

Until 1929 each church had its own parish priest and congregation. Today they come under one parish and the churchyard is separated by the Essex Way, a long distance path which stretches across Essex from Epping in the south-west to Harwich in the north-east. The churches are well worth visiting, and if you stroll through the churchyard you are in for a treat with magnificent views across the Roding Valley.

WILLINGALE

An American Air Base

During World War Two, Willingale buzzed with the sound of aircraft from the 387th Bombardment Division of the United States Army Air Force (USAAF). Officers were based at nearby Willingale Airfield, now abandoned; St Andrew's Church provided prayer and hope while the Bell public house, across the road, provided many a pint. With just over 500 people in the village and two pubs in which to socialise, Willingale was and still is, a pint-sized parish. But these days the village is distinctly 'dry' as the Bell and the Maltsers Arms are now private residences.

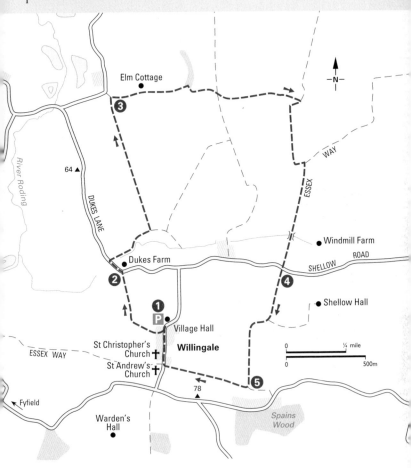

WALK 26 DIRECTIONS

❶ With your back to the village hall, turn right following the road around to the left and turn right at the footpath sign by the former village school, now a private residence. At the end of the gardens, keep ahead to the right of a hedge and follow the grassy path as it curves right, to reach Dukes Lane. To your left are panoramic views of the Roding Valley.

❷ Turn left into Dukes Lane and after passing a house called McKerros look out for where you turn right at a public footpath sign. Walk up the embankment and maintain direction along the

79

field-edge path with the stream on your right for about 400yds (366m). At a hedge gap on the right turn left along an uphill cross-field path, go over a plank footbridge by a hedge gap. Cross another field, a further footbridge and maintain direction until you reach the junction with Elms Farm Road on your left, and Elm Cottage over to the right.

WHILE YOU'RE THERE

St Andrew's Church, built of flint rubble with Roman tiles and reused bricks, dates from the 12th century but is no longer used for worship. Inside you can see some early 17th-century engraved brass memorial inscription plates, set in stone slabs on the chancel floor. Look for the Norman windows on the north and south walls and the ornate ironwork on the north door.

---

❸ Turn right on to the bridleway, pass Elm Cottage and continue for 1 mile (1.6km), ignoring a pair of footbridges. At the T-junction turn right along a track and at the next T-junction turn left and then right at the waymarked post to join the Essex Way. Follow this wide byway south, passing Windmill Farm on your left to reach Shellow Road.

❹ Cross the road and continue along the Essex Way, with views of Shellow Hall to your left. After 300yds (274m), cross a plank footbridge, turn right and later left, keeping the hedgerow to your right. After another 100yds (91m), turn right through the gap in the hedge, then continue with the hedgerow on your left.

❺ In front of the cottages at Spains Wood, cross the footbridge over the ditch and turn right, continuing along the Essex Way.

WHAT TO LOOK OUT FOR

Willingale has some lovely old houses, some of which can be seen on or near this walk. The Pound House dates back to the 17th century; Warden's Hall, to the south of the village, is a 16th-century red-brick house hiding behind an 18th-century façade. Keep an eye out also for the former pubs in the village which are now private houses as is the dairy and the old school house.

After an earth bridge, maintain direction keeping the hedgerow on your left. Follow the path through the cricket field and into Willingale where the Essex Way continues past The Bell on your right (now a private house) and crosses the churchyard between St Christopher's and St Andrew's churches. After exploring the churches and churchyard retrace your steps to The Street, which becomes Beech Road and return to the village hall car park.

WHERE TO EAT AND DRINK

There is nothing in Willingale itself, Fyfield is the nearest place for food and drink. Try The Queens Head for good pub lunches and snacks, and The Black Bull for home-cooked dishes and real ale. Otherwise, shop at Fyfield's Post Office and Stores or bring a packed lunch.

A Castle at Pleshey

*A gentle walk combining rolling countryside and
one of the finest motte-and-bailey castles in Britain.*

DISTANCE *3 miles (4.8km)*   MINIMUM TIME *1hr 30min*

ASCENT/GRADIENT *56ft (17m)* ▲▲▲   LEVEL OF DIFFICULTY ✦✦✦

PATHS *Grassy tracks, field and woodland paths
prone to muddiness, some roads*

LANDSCAPE *Gently rolling farmland, woodland and brook*

SUGGESTED MAP *OS Explorer 183 Chelmsford & The Rodings,
Maldon & Witham*

START / FINISH *Grid reference: TL 662142*

DOG FRIENDLINESS *Stacks of mud and lots of water to cool paws,
but should be on lead along fields*

PARKING *Free car park at the village hall*

PUBLIC TOILETS *None en route*

Long before the Norman conquest in 1066, Pleshey was occupied by
a Saxon settlement, but the village is better known for its motte-
and-bailey castle. William the Conqueror gave the land to Geoffrey de
Mandeville whose castle once crowned the towering, flat-topped grassy
mound, or motte, dominating the village and countryside. Constructed
from soil dug out to make a deep ditch, or moat, the motte was enclosed
by earth and timber stockades inside which was a wooden tower, later
replaced by one of stone. Here lived the Mandevilles, while the open area
in front of it, the bailey, or courtyard, was crammed with stables, barns
and storehouses. Today nothing remains of the castle apart from the 14th-
century brick bridge, believed to be the oldest in Britain.

The Tragic Fate of a Nobleman

Intrigue and heartbreak plagued Pleshey Castle. In 1142, Geoffrey de
Mandeville's grandson, also named Geoffrey, was arrested for his allegiance
to King Stephen's rival, Matilda. He secured his release by forfeiting Pleshey
and Saffron castles and the Tower of London, only to be killed two years
later. Eventually Pleshey passed to the Duke of Gloucester, who met his
fate at Calais in 1397, murdered on the orders of his nephew, Richard II,
who seized the castle and all his possessions. The Duchess of Gloucester
fled to a nunnery at Barking, but returned to Pleshey to die.

Pleshey, which over the centuries developed to the north of the motte
and bailey, is surrounded by a stream and a partly water-filled ditch known
as the Town Enclosure. Today the village, with its two pubs, 16th- and 17th-
century cottages and village hall, evokes a real sense of community. But like
many places throughout the country, Pleshey's castle, church and College
of Canons were seized by Henry VIII and given to a greedy kinsman, John
Gates. Gates destroyed everything, and only the earthworks and a few
arches in the church remind us of Pleshey's former glory.

PLESHEY

Peace and Public Houses

The walk takes in part of the Essex Way, a national recreational footpath, which slices through the village along The Street passing The White Horse pub and The Leather Bottle and follows Walthambury Brook. Take time to visit the interior of Holy Trinity Church where a stone on the wall, reputed to have come from Pleshey Castle, reads 'Ricardus Rex II', a reminder of its royal patronage. Next door is the country's first House of Retreat, owned by the Diocese of Chelmsford. A former convent, it played an important role as a convalescent home for Belgian soldiers injured in World War One, and today is a haven of peace and prayer welcoming all denominations.

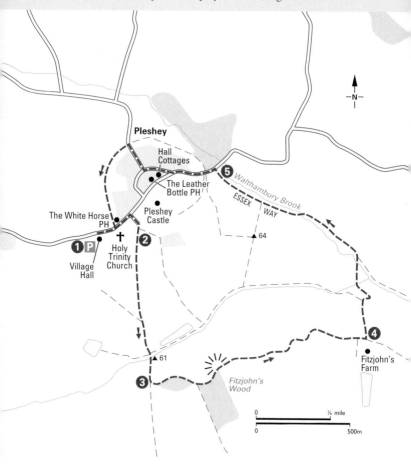

WALK 27 DIRECTIONS

❶ From the car park at the village hall, walk to The Street and turn right passing Holy Trinity Church on your right and The White Horse pub on your left. After the church you will see the 16th-century gatehouse, behind which is the convent, collectively they are known as the House of Retreat. Just after the restored water pump turn right into Pump Lane. After 100yds (91m), on your left you will see the bridge over the moat – the entrance into the earthworks of the motte-and-bailey castle.

PLESHEY

❷ With your back to the castle, and keeping the church to your right, walk across the cricket field to the waymark beside the wooden gate. Turn right along the concrete path keeping the field on your left. Maintain direction, ignoring two footpaths on the right and one on the left by the reservoir.

❸ At the three-way public footpath sign turn left and follow the bridleway bounded by trees. This path, which may be very muddy after rain, passes by Fitzjohn's Wood affording good views of rolling countryside. Beyond the outline of Holy Trinity Church you can appreciate the advantage of the hillside location of Pleshey Castle.

❹ When you are level with the old house on the right, which was Fitzjohn's Farm, walk a few paces to the line of trees by a waymark on your left and turn left on to the field-edge path, downhill. Just after a wooden footbridge

over a brook to your left the path curves first right and then left beside a wire fence. Keep ahead to cross a plank footbridge over Walthambury Brook and continue up the embankment so that the brook is now on your left. You are now on the grassy path of the Essex Way, which follows Walthambury Brook all the way to The Street at Pleshey.

❺ Turn left at The Street and turn right into Back Lane, passing Pleshey Hall Cottages on your left. At the signpost marked Pleshey Grange, turn right into Vicarage Road, passing the site of the former Pleshey Forge on your left. At the next public footpath sign, just after a house called Pleachfield, turn left on to the grassy path which follows the Town Enclosure, with the ditch on your left. Cross the footbridge and maintain direction until you reach The White Horse pub on your left and emerge into The Street. Turn right to return to the car park.

The Longer Ongar Walk

Rolling farmlands, big skies and a pretty Essex village where missionary David Livingstone lived and preached.

WALK 28

> **DISTANCE** 6.5 miles (10.4km) **MINIMUM TIME** 3hrs 30min
>
> **ASCENT/GRADIENT** 151ft (46m) ▲▲▲ **LEVEL OF DIFFICULTY** ✦✦✦
>
> **PATHS** Track and field paths prone to muddiness, stretches of road, 5 stiles
>
> **LANDSCAPE** Rolling farmland, patches of woodland, village streets
>
> **SUGGESTED MAP** OS Explorer 183 Chelmsford & The Rodings, Maldon & Witham and OS Explorer 175 Southend-on-Sea and Basildon
>
> **START / FINISH** Grid reference: TL 552032
>
> **DOG FRIENDLINESS** Larger, or older, dogs (and their owners) will find stiles quite difficult
>
> **PARKING** Pay-and-display car parks at rear of Sainsbury's, police station and library in Chipping Ongar High Street
>
> **PUBLIC TOILETS** Car park next to the police station

Chipping Ongar's most famous resident was explorer and missionary David Livingstone (1813–73). Born in Blantyre in Scotland he came from a simple working class background and as a 10-year-old worked at a cotton mill, finishing at the end of the day to bury himself in books. In 1836 he studied medicine in Glasgow, returning to the mill in the summer. At this time he attended a meeting by Dr Robert Moffat who ran a missionary station in Africa, and was inspired by his work there.

In 1838 Livingstone moved to Essex to extend his understanding of missionary work. He lived in a room near the United Reformed church in the High Street, Ongar, and in his spare time would take long walks in the countryside. Livingstone stayed in Ongar for 15 months before leaving for London to complete his medical studies. In 1840 the London Missionary Sociey sent him to Africa where he spent his life immersed in his missionary work, establishing trade routes and writing books about the great continent, where he discovered Victoria Falls in 1855.

During his time in Ongar, Livingstone walked to London to visit a sick relative but got hopelessly lost at Stanford Rivers. On another occasion, when standing in for his minister at the Independent Chapel at Stanford Rivers, Livingstone apparently forgot his sermon, panicked and fled from the congregation. This was the shy nervous individual who went on to become a world-famous explorer!

Churches and Farmland

Like Livingstone it's easy to get lost when exploring the muddy lanes around Ongar. On this walk you take the Essex Way, which is nicely waymarked, to Greensted and the oldest wooden church in the world. Livingstone would have walked around this delightful church discovering the crusader coffin in the churchyard and the original timbers, which archaeologists confirm date back to 1066. Thereafter you traverse

CHIPPING ONGAR

farmlands to Stanford Rivers climbing to a fine ridge of ancient oaks at Kettlebury Spring and views of rolling countryside. You finish your walk in the High Street and pass the room where Livingstone once lived.

That Famous Phrase

In 1871 a very sick Livingstone was found beside Lake Tanganyika by the American journalist Henry Morton Stanley who addressed him with the famous phrase, 'Dr Livingstone, I presume'. Stanley failed to convince Livingstone to return to England and he died in Africa two years later. No hack will be waiting but, as you emerge into the High Street after being ankle-deep in mud, the locals might just say, 'Essex walkers, I presume?'

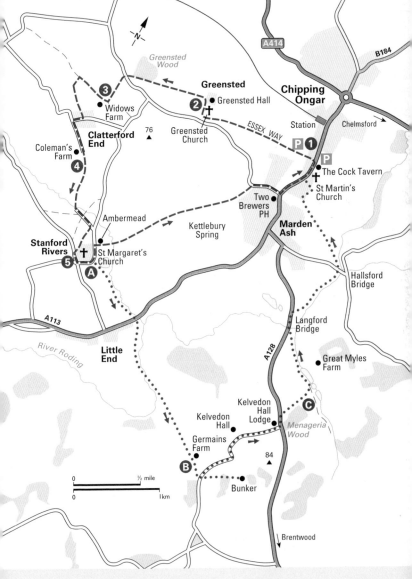

WALK 28 DIRECTIONS

1 From the rear of the car park beside the police station take the Essex Way towards Greensted. As the path narrows, walk between dwarf oaks, over the cross path and through the kissing gate and keep ahead, passing the pond of Greensted Hall on your right. Walk through the gate, passing Church Lodge on your left; Greensted church is on your right.

2 Keeping the church on your right, bear right towards a barn conversion and go through the waymarked gate. After 100yds (91m), turn left across the footbridge and follow the field-edge path keeping the hedgerow on your right. Maintain this direction through three fields, passing Greensted Wood on your right, until you reach Greensted Road. Turn left and pick up the footpath on your right. Continue along the field-edge path keeping hedgerows on your left for about 100yds (91m), where you go through a kissing-gate so that the hedgerow is now on your right. Negotiate a series of stiles and squeezer stiles.

3 At the fifth stile turn right, pass to the right of Widows Farm and continue along an enclosed path of The Essex Way. At a Y-junction of paths take the left path diagonally across the field to

a hedge. Keep the hedge on your left and continue ahead towards houses. Turn right along the lane and at T-junction turn left towards Coleman's Farm.

4 As the lane bears right into Coleman's Farm, maintain direction on to the bridleway for 0.5 mile (800m), ignoring paths left and right until you reach the tarmac lane. Just before the T-junction, turn right on to the cross-field path to Stanford Rivers. At the converted barn dwellings on your left, turn right on to the gravel path then left on to School Road with St Margaret's Church on your left.

5 Walk past the church to the crossroads and turn left. After 400yds (366m) follow the right turn next to the house called Ambermead. Maintain direction on the uphill path for views of farmland and pass the ridge of oak trees at Kettlebury Spring. Follow the path past the school and turn right to reach The Borough. Continue to the T-junction passing the Two Brewers pub on the right. Turn left into the High Street and return to the car park.

WALK 28

Cold War Kelvedon Hatch

A longer walk taking in a secret cold war bunker.

See map and information panel for Walk 28

DISTANCE *5.25 miles (8.4km)*	**MINIMUM TIME** *3hrs*	
ASCENT/GRADIENT *200ft (61m)* ▲▲▲	**LEVEL OF DIFFICULTY** ✦✦✦	

WALK 29 DIRECTIONS
(Walk 28 option)

After passing St Margaret's Church turn right at a public footpath sign. At a waymark sign, Point **A**, turn right and with the pond on your left, follow the path downhill. Just before a concrete bridge take the right-hand path with the brook on your left for 547yds (500m). Cross a plank footbridge at a hedge gap and keep ahead to a row of houses at Little End. Cross the A113 and the cattle grid. Just before a second cattle grid climb a stile on the right and continue for 0.25 mile (400m) then climb another stile on the left. Cross a concrete track and a footbridge over the River Roding. Follow the footpath for 1 mile (1.6km) to Germains Farm, Point **B**, and keep ahead, and go through a gate on to a gravel track to reach Kelvedon Hall Lane.

Ignore the 'private' sign and walk up to the entrance of the Kelvedon Hatch bunker. Built during the cold war, the three storeys were concealed 75ft (23m) below ground.

Retrace your steps to Kelvedon Hall Lane and turn right. Maintain direction along the road until you reach a T-junction, which emerges next to the grand Kelvedon Hall Lodge on the busy A128. Turn left, cross the road and turn right through the wide gap in the hedgerow. Walk ahead keeping Menageria Wood, Point **C**, on your right until you meet the cross path by three fishing lakes. From the red-brick bridge ahead there are pleasant views of the lakes and Great Myles Farm with its distinctive clock tower.

Do not cross the bridge but, keeping the lake on your right, follow the path for 0.5 mile (800m) to meet the A128 at Langford Bridge. Turn right and walk through a series of wooden gates over the bridge and, after 100yds (91m) take the footpath right, keeping the river to your right until you reach Hallsford Bridge. Cross the road, go over the stile and take the cross-field path half left towards the church spire on the hill. Pass houses on your left then cross the stream via the concrete bridge. Bear left to the kissing gate, walk down past a row of cottages in Bushey Lea and rejoin Walk 28 in Chipping Ongar High Street.

WHERE TO EAT AND DRINK

Kelvedon Hatch bunker lives up to its cold war fame. In those days it operated round the clock serving hot food for the bunker's personnel. Now it makes a great pit stop for walkers.

Overleaf: The attractive exterior of Greensted Church (Walk 28)

Bringing Home the Bacon at Little Dunmow

A short rural walk and how married couples compete for a side of bacon.

DISTANCE 3 miles (4.8km)   **MINIMUM TIME** 1hr 15min

ASCENT/GRADIENT 89ft (27m) ▲▲▲   **LEVEL OF DIFFICULTY** ✦✦✦

PATHS Grassy and farm tracks, field-edge paths liable to be muddy after rain

LANDSCAPE Disused railway track, riverside meadow and farm tracks

SUGGESTED MAP OS Explorer 195 Braintree & Saffron Walden

START / FINISH Grid reference: TL 655216

DOG FRIENDLINESS A nice frolic on Flitch Way but watch out for cyclists and keep on lead by fields

PARKING Informal street parking in Little Dunmow

PUBLIC TOILETS None en route

WALK 30 DIRECTIONS

The tiny village of Little Dunmow was the original home of an ancient ceremony known as the Dunmow Flitch Trial. A flitch, or side of bacon, was awarded to a married couple who could claim that they had lived in total peace and harmony for a year and a day. Nobody is sure how or why the ceremony came to be, but one theory is that the church authorities preferred couples to marry rather than live together as common law man and wife and a side of bacon, at a time when both food and money were scarce, provided an edible bonus. Winning such a prize in those days was equivalent to winning today's national lottery and one enterprising couple made a tidy profit by carving off slices to sell to hungry sightseers!

The ceremony fell out of favour by the mid-18th century but was revived in 1855, thanks to a publicity stunt by novelist Harrison Ainsworth (1805–82). His book, *The Flitch of Bacon* was a hit the year before, and in an effort to cash in on its success, he was instrumental in arranging for the Flitch Trial to be moved from Little Dunmow to Great Dunmow. Presiding as judge he awarded a flitch of bacon to an Ongar builder and his wife and, ever since, the Flitch Trial has been held at Great Dunmow every leap year.

Park outside the Flitch of Bacon pub. With your back to the pub turn right and right again into Grange Lane and turn left towards

WHAT TO LOOK FOR

Inside Little Dunmow's church is the tomb of Walter Fitzwalter, a descendant of Robert Fitzwalter, lord of the manor, and some believe the founder of the Dunmow Flitch Trial. You can also see the oak chair in which successful claimants of the Flitch of Bacon were enthroned each year, and medieval Latin graffiti which translates as 'a short life and a merry one.'

LITTLE DUMNOW

WALK 30

the church at the public footpath sign. Continue past a row of houses at the fingerpost. Bear right, pass the Church of St Mary the Virgin on your left, and follow the yellow waymarks to join the Flitch Way.

The church is all that remains of the old Augustinian priory of Little Dunmow and its main claim to fame is its association with the Flitch Trial. Founded in the 12th century it was, like other religious houses, dissolved by Henry VIII in 1536. As you leave the church you pass Priory Place. This house was one of several which belonged to the priory, beyond it is the site of the priory fishponds. These were kept well stocked to provide food, but there is no record of a Flitch fish trial.

Go through a kissing gate and turn right on to the Flitch Way a 15-mile (24km) linear nature park occupying the site of the old Bishop's Stortford-to-Braintree

railway line. Today high hedgerows on either side of the railway form a canopy full of wildlife. The line opened in 1869 and provided services for passengers, farmers and local industries who transported goods to main towns along the route. Passenger services stopped in 1952 and the line was eventually closed down in 1969.

Follow the Flitch Way for 1 mile (1.6km) and look out for where you turn right at a metal barrier before the metal and brick bridge. At a set of waymarks turn right, away from the bridge, along an uphill track. Continue along this meandering path to the right of the A120 to pass Clobbs Cottage.

At the T-junction turn right away from the footbridge over the A120. The path later passes to the left of Little Dunmow's church.

At the T-junction turn left into The Street where you will see an old red water pump on the left just before the Flitch of Bacon pub. This was erected in 1887 to mark Queen Victoria's Jubilee by Warners, a foundry that made many village pumps as well as bells and carillons. Continue to the pub for a well-earned rest.

Around Great Bardfield

An easy stroll combining gentle hills, a windmill called Gibraltar and the stronghold of a royal solicitor.

DISTANCE *4.5 miles (7.2km)* **MINIMUM TIME** *2hrs*

ASCENT/GRADIENT *100ft (30m)* ▲▲▲ **LEVEL OF DIFFICULTY** ✦✦✦

PATHS *Field-edge paths, river bank, grassy tracks and some town streets, 4 stiles*

LANDSCAPE *Undulating grazing, arable farmland and river valley*

SUGGESTED MAP *OS Explorer 195 Braintree & Saffron Walden*

START / FINISH *Grid reference: TL 677305*

DOG FRIENDLINESS *A lot of places, including sheep fields, where dogs must be on lead*

PARKING *Informal parking in Great Bardfield village*

PUBLIC TOILETS *None en route*

Every so often you come across a delightful Essex village which begs to be explored. Great Bardfield is one such village, but there is nothing large about it. Quite the contrary, it is tiny but what it lacks in size is compensated by the sheer loveliness of the village itself and the surrounding countryside. The village is sited on a wide, gently sloping High Street with an attractive green overlooked by St Mary's Church, noted for its rare 14th-century stone rood screen, while a brick-built bridge across the River Pant links Great Bardfield with Finchingfield to the north.

A Generous Benefactor

Great Bardfield owes much of its heritage to William Bendlowes. He was born in the village in 1516 and went on to become Sergeant-at-Law to Mary Tudor and Queen Elizabeth I. He lived at Place House, one of the most historically important houses in the village, and died there in 1564. At Place House, it is said, Queen Elizabeth sought sanctuary from the persecution of her sister. Whether this is a story which got better with each telling is difficult to know, but what is indisputable is that Bendlowes left much of his wealth to the village.

Bendlowes was buried alongside his wife, Alienor, in St Mary's Church where his family later donated the chancel roof in 1618. He left a charitable trust and as you walk around the village you will see his legacy everywhere. There are cottage almshouses near the High Street; the Cottage Museum is another almshouse, inhabited until 1958, but now owned by the Bendlowes Trust and run by the local historical society. Bendlowes and his wife would have admired the countryside hereabouts with its gentle hills, but would not have seen the windmill, incongruously named Gibraltar. Built in 1660, it last saw service as a mill in the 1930s, and is now a private residence overlooking pleasant Essex fields.

Farmworkers and farmers alike from Champions, Robjohns and Whinbush farms would have trudged along footpaths to get to church while the occupants of Bardfield Hall would have only needed to walk next door. These farms today have been modernised, while Bardfield Hall, now a picturesque private residence, retains many of its 16th-century features.

Great Bardfield didn't feature on the itinerary of long haul carriages from Newmarket to London but that is not to say that the village was devoid of pubs. In the early 19th century when a brawl took place in one of the village's three inns and the miscreants needed a place to cool off, the village lock up in Bridge Street would have provided spartan accommodation for a handful of prisoners in its two tiny cells.

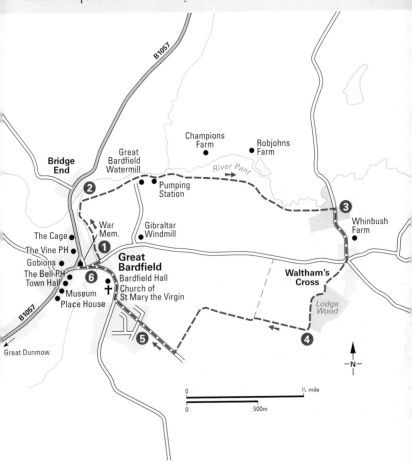

WALK 31 DIRECTIONS

❶ From the war memorial opposite The Vine pub walk down the hill passing the Quaker Meeting House to the village green. Turn left at the public footpath sign, follow the path by the public footpath sign and then follow the path by the stream on

your left with houses on your right. After 200yds (183m) at the field, take the left fork still following the stream. Look over your right shoulder for a very good view of Gibraltar Windmill.

❷ Cross the stile through the hedge, turn right and continue with the hedge on your right until you reach the lane at Great Bardfield Watermill. Cross the lane and keep the mill pond and the River Pant on your left and pass to the left of a pumping station. Go over a stile and take the cross-field path keeping the river and Champions Farm and Robjohns Farm on your left. Cross an earth bridge and stay on the grassy path through arable farmland keeping the river on your left-hand side and crossing a footbridge by a waymark post and a stile. Go through a gate and cross a stile to reach a lane.

3 Turn right uphill passing Whinbush Farm. When you reach the junction of the Bardfield–Waltham road, bear right following a green public footpath sign. Cross two stiles and maintain your direction along the path which skirts the edge of Lodge Wood. Go over another stile and after 100yds (91m) look

out for where you turn right at a waymark. Keeping the wood on your left, continue to another waymark and turn right beside a hedgerow.

4 Follow the path by the hedge under the row of poplar and larch trees and, as the outline of Great Bardfield and the windmill come into view, turn left. Follow the track with hedgerows on your left for about 300yds (274m) and turn right into the green lane.

5 Walk past the recreation ground on your right, cross the residential street and follow the footpath into Braintree Road where you turn right. On your left is the Church of St Mary the Virgin with its Norman tower and 14th-century nave. Local benefactors, the Bendlowes family, are buried inside the church.

6 Next to the church is the 16th-century manor house of Bardfield Hall, and for a further taste of Great Bardfield's history follow the road left through Brook Street, passing the starting point of the walk into the High Street. In quick succession you can see Gobions, one of the oldest houses in the village, Place House, the Cottage Museum and the Town Hall. After some refreshment retrace your steps to the green.

The Sound of Music at Thaxted

*A glorious country walk following in the footsteps
of composer Gustav Holst.*

DISTANCE 3 miles (4.8km)   **MINIMUM TIME** 1hr 30min

ASCENT/GRADIENT 92ft (28m) ▲▲▲   **LEVEL OF DIFFICULTY** ✦✦✦

PATHS Field-edge paths, bridleway prone to muddiness,
river bank and some town streets

LANDSCAPE Arable fields, meadows and undulating farmland

SUGGESTED MAP OS Explorer 195 Braintree & Saffron Walden

START / FINISH Grid reference: TL 610311

DOG FRIENDLINESS Great for romping

PARKING Free car park at Margaret Street

PUBLIC TOILETS Car park in Margaret Street

Thaxted must be one of Essex's prettiest villages, the sort you would expect to find gracing the top of a chocolate box, with its picturesque windmill, delightful thatched houses and a guildhall dating back to the 13th century. Perhaps this is what attracted composer and musician Gustav Holst (1874–1934) to the village. The young Gustav stayed overnight in Thaxted in 1913 during a five-day winter walking holiday in north-west Essex, little knowing that a few years later he would come here to live.

An Inspiring View

Home for the composer, his wife and their daughter was, at first, a 17th-century thatched cottage. From here there were views across meadows and willow trees to the magnificent spire of St John the Baptist church in the village and this view, coupled with tranquillity and solitude, provided the inspiration for his work, *The Planets Suite* (1914–16).

Holst was born in Cheltenham to a father who came from the Baltic port of Riga. When he came to Thaxted he was known as Gustav von Holst, a name which at first aroused suspicion amongst the villagers who couldn't understand what motivated this stranger to walk for so long and so far. On this walk you will enjoy panoramas of rolling countryside and big skies, and see the soaring spire of the church, visible for miles around, and perhaps experience similar feelings of liberation as the young Gustav whose genius was to make him one of our greatest composers.

Turbulent Priest

Holst became great friends with the local vicar, the socialist Father Conrad Noel, a colourful and controversial character who called him 'Our Mr Von'. Noel upset the villagers one day in 1921 by hoisting Sinn Fein and communist red flags above the church. To add fuel to the fire he deliberately omitted hoisting the Union Jack believing it to be a flag of imperialist oppression. Angry Cambridge students tore down the flags and replaced them with the Union Jack, an act which drove the vicar

quite wild. A pitched battle ensued with Noel and his followers slashing the tyres of the demonstrators' cars and motorbikes until order was fully restored by the church authorities.

Summer Music Festival

In calmer times Holst played the church organ, helped local singers and brought London students to the parish church where they sang Bach cantatas. At Christmas he sang carols and invited the choir to his home at the Manse in Town Street, where a plaque commemorates his residence here. Holst died in 1934 and he is remembered with a month-long summer music festival in Thaxted, which attracts performers worldwide.

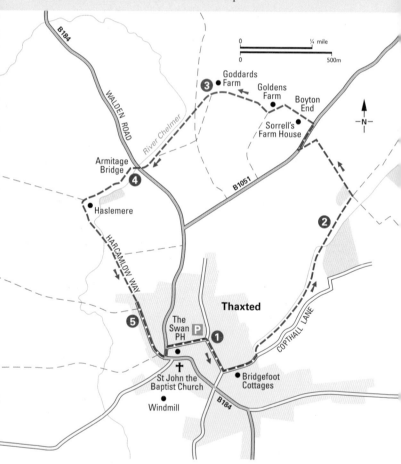

WALK 32 DIRECTIONS

❶ From the car park turn left into Margaret Street, right into Weaverhead Lane and left into Copthall Lane, passing the row of cottages called Bridgefoot. After the houses on your left, pass

through the gap between trees by the gate marked Walnut Tree Meadow. Turn right along the grassy path and keep parallel with Copthall Lane on your right. After 400yds (366m) bear left at the yellow waymark through trees, cross two footbridges at right angles, in quick succession, and turn right keeping the stream and hedgerows on your right.

❷ Maintain direction along the field-edge path through two fields. After the spinney on your left, turn left at the waymark over the footbridge and follow another field-edge path keeping the hedgerow on your left and crossing another footbridge to the B1051, Sampford Road. In the distance, to your left is the spire of St John the Baptist Church. Turn right, cross the road with care, and take the first turning on the left along the farm track marked Boyton End. The track zig-zags left and right past Sorrell's Farm House and Goldens Farm. At Golden Farm bear right on to the narrow canopied bridleway between buildings, and later bear right along a field-edge. Turn left outside Goddards Farm and follow the track downhill.

❸ Cross a road to the farm and the adjacent track to follow a fingerpost through the hedge. Turn half left across the field and follow the path with the River Chelmer on your right to Walden Road.

❹ At Walden Road turn right across Armitage Bridge and immediately left at the public footpath sign (now following

Turpin's Trail). Follow the field-edge path with the river on your left passing conifers and, after 300yds (274m), turn left at the waymark concealed in the hedgerows. You are now on the Harcamlow Way. Continue downhill along a driveway leading from the house called Haslemere, and go over concrete bridge across the river. Ignore paths left and right and continue along the tarmac road, past some elegant modern housing surrounded by rolling countryside.

❺ Continue along Watling Lane passing 17th-century cottages and Piggot's Mill until you emerge opposite The Swan. Turn left and right into Margaret Street and return to the car park.

From Saffron Walden

A fairly challenging walk along part of the Harcamlow Way to Audley End, taking in beautiful rolling countryside.

WALK 33

DISTANCE 5.5 miles (8.8km)   **MINIMUM TIME** 2hrs 30min

ASCENT/GRADIENT 180ft (55m) ▲▲▲   **LEVEL OF DIFFICULTY** +++

PATHS Urban, field-edge, grassy tracks

LANDSCAPE Downland, arable farmland, grassy meadow and woodland

SUGGESTED MAP OS Explorer 195 Braintree & Saffron Walden

START / FINISH Grid reference: TL 534384

DOG FRIENDLINESS Mostly on lead

PARKING Long stay at Swan Meadow.

PUBLIC TOILETS Swan Meadow

Saffron Walden is a picturesque medieval town. Originally known as Walden meaning 'valley of the Welsh' (ie Britons), the town's distinctive prefix was added in the 15th century when many parts of north-west Essex began growing the saffron crocus and the town became a centre of trade for saffron. Every autumn the flowers were picked by hand and brought to the town where the chive, or stigma, was removed, dried and then sold.

Saffron was mainly used for dyeing although a few Waldenians seem to have used it as a spice or medicine. By the early 1700s saffron production fell into decline mainly due to cheaper imports from Spain and the Middle East. However, the saffron flower symbol can be seen on the decorative plasterwork, or pargetting, on the Old Sun Inn in Church Street, inside the parish church and on the coat-of-arms on the Town Hall.

On this walk you can imagine what the surrounding countryside to the west of Saffron Walden must have looked like when it was covered with crocus blooms. We leave the town passing the Edward VI almshouses (1834), which provided homes for the poor, and walk along Abbey Lane to enter the wrought iron gates of Audley End Park. This great park extends from Saffron Walden to the Cambridge road and Audley End House, which stands on the site of the former Benedictine monastery of Walden Abbey.

Historic House and Fine Parkland

Audley End House was given to Sir Thomas Audley in 1538 by Henry VIII. It was used as a private residence but demolished and rebuilt by his grandson, Thomas Howard, 1st Earl of Suffolk, as a much grander mansion for entertaining James I. A story tells that Thomas Howard lied to the King saying he had spent £200,000 on creating the house and that the King had unwittingly contributed to the cost. In 1619 both Howard and his wife were locked up in the Tower of London for fraud but payment of a huge fine set them free and seven years later, Howard died in disgrace at Audley End. Today the house is a third of its original size but it is still very grand. We pass through the one-street hamlet of Audley End and its row of cottages, where the estate workers lived, before returning to town.

Right: Stained glass in the parish church at Saffron Walden

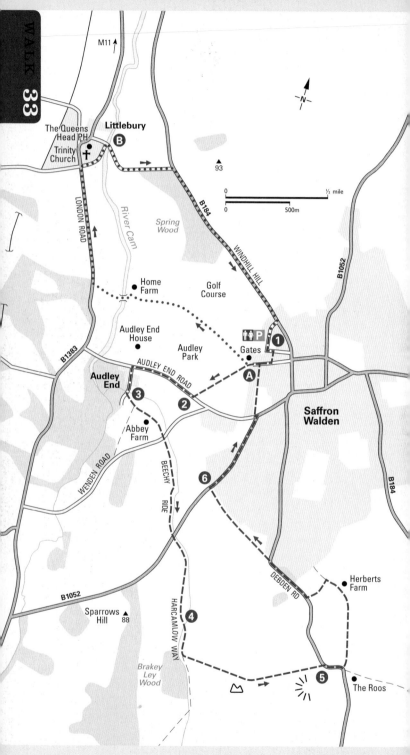

Right: The façade of Audley End House

WALK 33 DIRECTIONS

1 From Swan Meadow car park follow the 'town centre' sign into Park Lane turning right to go through a small archway of the almshouses. Turn right into Abbey Lane and go through the wrought iron gates of Audley End Park. Maintain direction along the grassy path to the top of the hill, and exit via another set of wrought iron gates, to Audley End Road.

2 Turn right along the embankment and go downhill for 600yds (549m), keeping the red brick wall of Audley End Park on your right, until you reach the fingerpost marked 'College of St Mark'. Cross the road and turn left to Audley End village.

3 Cross the bridge and turn left at the lane marked 'Abbey Farm private' and continue along this footpath keeping St Mark's College, followed by the farm, to your right. Maintain direction along the concrete drive, cross Wenden Road and go through trees to join Beechy Ride (track). Keep the stream and line of beech trees to your right for 200yds (183m), until you cross the earth bridge between the trees, and continue with the stream and trees to your left to the B1052. Cross the road with care, and continue along the footpath opposite, along the edge of a field with the stream on your left. At the earth bridge turn left and immediately right so that the stream is now on your right.

4 Follow the field-edge path until it abuts Brakey Ley Wood and ignore the three sets of waymarks indicating right turns. At the fourth waymark, continue along the field-edge path to Debden Road.

5 Turn right at Debden Road and, opposite The Roos, turn left on to a byway and then immediately left along the uphill path. Bear left at Herberts Farm and left again to rejoin Debden Road. Turn right towards Claypits Plantation and maintain direction into Seven Devil Lane.

6 After 0.5 mile (800m) turn right on the B1052 towards Saffron Walden. At the roundabout bear left across the road and follow the footpath between houses later passing a deep ditch on the left, which is part of ancient defence system. At the end of the path turn right into Abbey Lane and the car park.

Around Audley End

*A short loop walk from Audley End Park
via Littlebury to Saffron Walden.*

See map and information panel for Walk 33

DISTANCE 3 miles (4.8km) **MINIMUM TIME** 1hr 15min
ASCENT/GRADIENT 123ft (37m) ▲▲▲ **LEVEL OF DIFFICULTY** ✦✦✦

WALK 34 DIRECTIONS
(Walk 33 option)

After passing through the entrance gate to Audley Park, Point **A**, turn right on to the path across grassland and after 200yds (183m) cross the footbridge and maintain direction, with the stream and golf course on your right. Look to your left for views of Audley End House before reaching the Tudor brickwork stables roofs.

Audley End House dates back to the early 17th century when it was much grander than the mansion we see today. Part of it was demolished because successive owners couldn't afford its upkeep. In the 18th century Lord Braybrook ordered its refurbishment by the architect Vanbrugh. Robert Adam was the interior designer and 'Capability' Brown was the landscape genius.

At the gate to a farm track on your right, turn left. Cross two bridges over the River Cam and continue uphill to the B1383. Turn right and walk along the verge towards Littlebury for 0.5 mile (800m). Turn right into Mill Lane, passing Trinity Church on your left, followed by weather-boarded cottages and a converted mill, to the T-junction, Point **B**.

Littlebury's claim to fame is the joke house built by Henry Winstanley, who also built Eddystone Lighthouse in 1698. He was born in Saffron Walden in 1644 and died in his own lighthouse in 1703. Winstanley lived near Trinity Church and would subject his houseguests to practical jokes, which included getting them to use a joke armchair, which wouldn't allow the sitter to get up.

Turn right into Walden Road and cross Littlebury Bridge over the River Cam. After 500yds (457m), turn right on to the B184, Windmill Hill. This is a busy road into Saffron Walden and the site of a Bronze Age settlement. You can walk safely along the raised embankment passing the flint walls of Spring Wood on your right. Walk for 0.75 mile (1.2km) and turn right into New Pond Lane passing Saffron Walden Golf Club to return to Swan Meadow car park.

WHAT TO LOOK FOR
Swan Meadow was a swampy place and was left as overgrown grassland. As a result it became a rare wet pasture habitat for birds. It became a car park in 1992, but some nature thrives in the nearby pond.

Saffron Walden Town

*A stroll taking in the architectural splendours
of a country market town.*

DISTANCE 3.5 miles (5.7km)   MINIMUM TIME 1hr 30 min

ASCENT/GRADIENT 62ft (19m) ▲▲▲   LEVEL OF DIFFICULTY ✦✦✦

PATHS Urban, parkland and common

LANDSCAPE Country town architecture

SUGGESTED MAP OS Explorer 195 Braintree & Saffron Walden

START / FINISH Grid reference: TL 540385

DOG FRIENDLINESS On lead all the way, though maze is dog friendly

PARKING Pay-and-display at Swan Meadow, Common Hill and
Fairycroft Road, free parking at Catons Lane

PUBLIC TOILETS Swan Meadow, Common Hill and Fairycroft

WALK 35 DIRECTIONS

Saffron Walden is a delightful
country town and well worth
a visit at any time of the year.
In 1968, it was designated a
Conservation Area, unsurprising
perhaps when you consider that
the town has some 400 buildings
of special architectural or historic
interest dating back to medieval
times. There are houses with
massive timbers, carved brackets,
overhanging eaves and plastered
decorative fronts, or pargetting,
and a fine church looks boldly
across the town. Other attractions
include two mazes and lovely
gardens, the remains of a Norman
castle and some great walking
country right on its doorstep.
This trail explores part of the
Conservation Area but you should
allow time to wander at will and
lap up the atmosphere of this
picturesque town.

With your back to Common Hill
car park walk across The Common
to The Maze. The Common,
formerly Castle Green, which

played host to a Royal Tournament
in 1252, is nowadays a pleasant
recreational venue for local fairs
and festivals. At the far end is
The Maze, believed to be more
than 800 years old and reputed
to be the largest turf maze in the
country. If you have time you
can enjoy exploring its mile-long
(1.6km) trail before continuing
the town walk.

At The Maze, turn right to the
river and right again, keeping the
river on your left to head back to
the car park. At the car park turn
left then right into Hill Street,
turn right into Market Street

WHERE TO EAT AND DRINK

There are plenty of pubs,
restaurants, coffee shops and
take-aways to choose from. The
Kings Arms, a cosy pub dating
back to Tudor times in the heart
of the town, is a good place for
home-cooked food and real ales.
Cafe Cou Cou in George Street
serves healthy, home-made food,
including delicious fruity flapjacks.

SAFFRON WALDEN

passing Market Row on your left into Market Square. This is the hub of the town. The mock-Tudor Town Hall, with a projecting gable, houses the tourist office. Other notable buildings include the Italianate-style Corn Exchange, now the library, and an impressive drinking fountain commemorating the marriage between the Prince of Wales and Princess Alexandra in 1863.

Keeping the Corn Exchange on your left, walk towards Church Street to the historic Old Sun Inn, part of which is now a second-hand bookshop. This is where Cromwell is said to have stayed during the Civil War. This group of 14th-century houses is decorated with impressive 17th-century pargetting. Turn left into Church Street and right into the churchyard of St Mary the Virgin.

St Mary the Virgin, with its saffron crocus emblem, is one of the largest parish churches in Essex. Standing on the site of a Saxon and Norman church it was mostly rebuilt between 1450 and 1525 and its sheer size demonstrates the prosperity of the area.

At the church, turn right, cross Museum Street to view the museum and the ruined flint walls of the 11th-century castle keep, built on the remains of a Saxon church. Retrace your steps to Museum Street, turn right and then left into Castle Street. After passing house No 23 turn right into Bridge End Garden, past the Fry Art Gallery, and the town's other maze. This garden exudes Victorian elegance with a viewing platform, pavilions and statues.

Take the main path left into Bridge Street. Turn left to pass the 16th-century Eight Bells pub, with its fine carved beam decorated with leaves and dolphins below a downstairs window. Maintain direction towards the town crossing Castle Street, where on the right you can see the finest 15th-century medieval building in Saffron Walden. A former maltings, and one of six which graced the town in the 1600s, it's now the Youth Hostel and must be one of the most atmospheric places to stay in the county. Diagonally opposite this is the 16th-century house called The Close, home of Francis Gibson, creator of Bridge End Garden.

Continue along Bridge Street to see more listed buildings, one of which is is the Cross Keys Hotel, with a raised roof which was added in the 18th century. Turn left into King Street and right into the Rows, the town's medieval shopping centre, where the buildings still retain their 15th-century shop windows. Go left into Market Row to return to the car park.

Lambourne End to Chigwell

A challenging walk combining an ancient forest, a village immortalised by Dickens and panoramic views of the London skyline.

DISTANCE 9 miles (14.5km)	**MINIMUM TIME** 3hrs 30 min
ASCENT/GRADIENT 148ft (45m) ▲▲▲	**LEVEL OF DIFFICULTY** +++

PATHS Forest tracks, field-edge paths, green lanes, some streets, numerous stiles

LANDSCAPE Forest, meadows, fields and some urban streets

SUGGESTED MAP OS Explorer 174 Epping Forest & Lee Valley

START / FINISH Grid reference: TQ 478943

DOG FRIENDLINESS Lots of big stiles, but water bowl at Kings Head

PARKING Three free car parks along Manor Road in Hainault Forest

PUBLIC TOILETS Hainault Forest Country Park visitor centre (not en route)

Hainault Forest was once part of the royal forest which stretched right across Essex. Like the forests of Epping and Hatfield, deer were bred here to supply the royal table, but the forest is also famous for being the stamping ground of a rather infamous character, Dick Turpin (1705–39). This legendary highwayman probably had a hand in the business of poaching deer and whatever else he could lay his hands on, before turning his talents to the less risky pursuits of housebreaking and robbery.

A Life of Crime

Born in a pub in Hempstead, the young Dick started his working life as a butcher in Whitechapel. One day, when caught in the act of cattle rustling, he fled to deepest Essex, only to resurface as a small-time smuggler, thief and highwayman. The business of travel in Turpin's time was no mean feat, for who knew when he or his cronies would strike as those brave enough made the journey through Hainault Forest? When a job was done, Turpin would call at Ye Old Kings Head in Chigwell for a quick pint, pick up details of when the next coach was due and plan his next crime. After a life of highway robbery and murder he was hung at York, but it was thanks to Harrison Ainsworth's novel, *Rookwood* (1834), in which a description of his supposed epic ride from Westminster to York caught the popular imagination, that Turpin was transformed into a glamorous character.

In the forest it is not difficult to picture a masked highwayman galloping through misty woodlands of weirdly sculpted trees to Chigwell Row, with its delightful church and collection of characterful hostelries. In the area around east London there are many pubs called the Black Horse in honour of Turpin's steed, Black Bess, but it is at Ye Old Kings Head at Chigwell where, it is said, the rogue secreted his pistols inside the walls. They have not been found, neither has the cellar tunnel connected to Chigwell church across the road, which he used to escaped his pursuers.

Relish the atmosphere of this old Tudor pub which Charles Dickens (1812–70) described as the Maypole in *Barnaby Rudge* (1841). Of Ye Old Kings Head he wrote that it had 'more gable-ends than a lazy man would care to count on a sunny day'. As you walk across the rolling countryside, particularly between Chigwell and Lambourne End, a superb London skyline with Canary Wharf in the distance reveals itself. And although it's said that the ghost of Dick Turpin riding Black Bess appears twice a week, he won't trouble you as long as you keep to the marked paths…

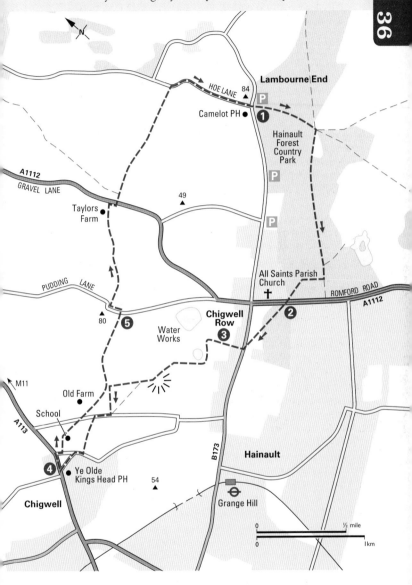

WALK 36 DIRECTIONS

❶ From the car park opposite the Miller & Carter pub walk straight along the wide bridleway between high trees. There is little forest floor covering and to the left you can see deep ancient woodland. After 350yds (320m) at the three-way fingerpost, turn right on to footpath No 43 towards Hainault. This stone chipping path runs

CHIGWELL

parallel with the bridleway on your left. Pass a public footpath signpost and 100yds (91m) after the second one signposted 'Retreat Path' turn right, go through a kissing gate and skirt the edge of the wood. Go through another kissing gate, bear right and walk parallel to the road to reach another kissing gate.

2 Cross Romford Road and go through a kissing gate opposite. Bear right to join the London Loop path through woodland and a recreation ground. Cross Manor Road and into Chapel Lane and take the narrow path between houses to the small meadow.

3 Maintain direction across four stiles and at the iron fence turn left along the path, keeping the waterworks behind the fencing to your right. Cross the concrete path at the waterworks' gate, and continue beside the fencing. At the break in the hedgerow on your left there are views of rolling countryside. Turn left at the waymarked fingerpost and follow the cross-field path downhill. Bear right at the next fingerpost and keep ahead, crossing a brook, and staying to the left of the hedgerow to reach a track. Turn left and continue along the field-edge path. Turn right on to the green lane and walk uphill with the Old Farm buildings to the right. Just before Old Farm turn left across a field, turn right and cross Vicarage Lane. After 150yds (137m) turn left on the path emerging on Chigwell High Road.

4 Turn right and right again, back into Vicarage Lane. Turn immediately left on to the cross-field path. Then bear right passing the primary school on your right. Follow the fingerpost diagonally across two fields, and maintain

## WHERE TO EAT AND DRINK

There is a good choice of pubs and most have plenty of character. Top of the bill has to be Ye Old Kings Head at Chigwell, immortalised by Dickens in *Barnaby Rudge*. The Miller & Carter steakhouse pub and grill's elevated position in Manor Road, overlooking beautiful countryside, makes a convenient and attractive stop beside the car park.

direction downhill crossing two stiles and the footbridge. Turn left and left again through the hedgerow then right, on to the field-edge path uphill. Cross a stile, continue to the left of the hedgerow, and go through a gate to the road.

5 Cross Pudding Lane and follow the public footpath sign on the field-edge path keeping Pudding Lane on your left. Take the cross-field path right gently downhill and emerge by Taylors Farmhouse. Turn right to emerge on to Gravel Lane. Cross the road, go over the stile opposite to Taylors Cottages and continue uphill, passing through the gap in the hedge to the right. Maintain direction to Hoe Lane and turn right to return to the car park.

WHILE YOU'RE THERE

If the Chigwell Show is taking place while you are here – usually the last weekend in August – head along to the Metropolitan Police Chigwell Sports Club in Chigwell High Road. Set in more than 40 acres (16ha), the Grade II listed mansion dates from the 1876 and the grounds have sweeping views over London.

Old and New Come Together at Harlow

A leisurely stroll exploring town and country from Mark Hall to Old Harlow.

DISTANCE *4 miles (6.4km)*   MINIMUM TIME *1hr 30min*

ASCENT/GRADIENT *67ft (20m)* ▲▲▲   LEVEL OF DIFFICULTY +++

PATHS *Cycle tracks, footpaths, sections of road, 1 stile*

LANDSCAPE *Urban, undulating farmland dotted with woodland*

SUGGESTED MAP *OS Explorer 174 Epping Forest & Lee Valley*

START / FINISH *Grid reference: TL 465109*

DOG FRIENDLINESS *Mainly on lead but can stretch legs in meadows*

PARKING *Free car park at Harlow Museum off Fesants Croft, open Tuesday to Sunday. Otherwise plenty of on-street parking*

PUBLIC TOILETS *Harlow Museum*

In 1944 Harlow was one of 32 locations around London selected as a site for a new town. On the western edge of Essex, the area consisted of a few scattered hamlets and farms and, apart from the villages of Old Harlow and Potter Street, it was rural and undeveloped with many fine trees and woodlands. Although close to London, Harlow was never intended to be a satellite of the capital, but a self-contained town with its own amenities to house Londoners whose homes had been destroyed in World War Two.

A Network of Cycle Tracks

Eminent architect Sir Frederick Gibberd proposed that the new town should be just west of the original village of Old Harlow. It was to consist of a central civic area surrounded by four large neighbourhood clusters, each with its own shops, churches, library, medical and community centres and schools. The clusters would be separated by wide green areas carrying the town's main roads. The woodland areas were increased by planting many thousands of trees, thus enhancing Harlow's rural atmosphere. In and around Harlow you will discover an independent system of cycle tracks, some former medieval lanes, which conserve the landscape and provide a link with the past.

The Museum

This walk starts from Mark Hall North, the first residential area to be built by Sir Frederick in 1953, and continues to the rural setting of Old Harlow, Mulberry and Churchgate Street in the east. In the 1950s many people cycled to work and these lanes are pedestrian-friendly, including the one we take near the Museum of Harlow, which is an extension of the original lane running from the centre of the new town to Old Harlow. Many old buildings nestle happily alongside the modern housing developments and the countryside reaches right into the centre thus earning its 'green town' reputation. On this route you will see Old Harlow, walk through the site of a Roman settlement, now a recreational park, and pass the medieval chapel of Harlowbury before reaching Churchgate Street with its delightful church and pubs backed by rural landscapes.

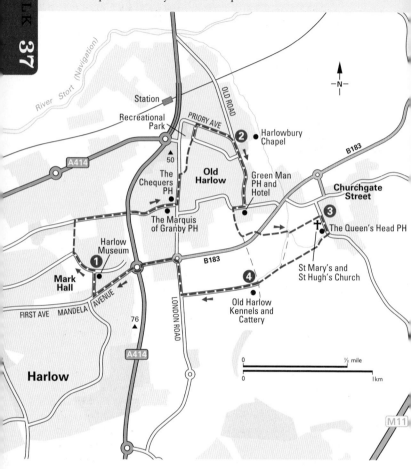

WALK 37 DIRECTIONS

❶ Turn left outside Harlow Museum, continue along Muskham Road and follow the blue cycle path sign to Templefields and Old Harlow. Turn right and follow the cycle path under the A414 and into Old Harlow. Continue along Market Street to the T-junction and turn left at The Chequers pub into Station Road. After 300yds (274m), turn right into the Swallows estate, take the first left and follow the footpath through

the recreational park to Manor Road. Turn left then right into Priory Avenue passing a row of corporation houses, the first to be built in the early days of Harlow new town, until you come to the crossroads with Old Road.

❷ Turn right and to your left you can see 12th-century Harlowbury Chapel worked in flint and rubble, but for better views walk another 150yds (137m) along Old Road to the kissing gate. This Norman chapel is a Grade I listed building and thought to be the oldest intact building in Harlow. It still has some original features including three windows. Maintain direction until you reach the T-junction opposite the Green Man pub and hotel. Here turn right and take the footpath between the old ambulance and fire station and walk the field-edge path. Just before the main road, turn left between concrete posts and follow the footpath to the B183. Bear half left, cross the road and follow the footpath through trees and bear left on to the field-edge path. After 200yds (183m), cross the stile and the footbridge and walk towards the spire of St Mary's and St Hugh's Church to arrive at the graveyard and continue ahead through the churchyard.

❸ Turn right into Churchgate Street passing the 17th-century Widow's House – inscribed with a dedication by a landowner's wife to a pair of poor widows –

followed by The Queen's Head pub and other timber-framed houses. Continue downhill to the footpath on the right just before the Swallow Churchgate Hotel. Cross the bridge and keeping the church and stream on your right, follow the field-edge path to pass a barrier. Bear half left across the meadow through the break in the fence opposite beside a redundant stile and, keeping the trees and stream on your right, continue to the kissing gate at the top of the hill.

❹ Pass the outbuildings of the Old Harlow Kennels and Cattery on your left and follow the tarmac road to London Road. Turn right into London Road and cross just before the roundabout on to the B183 to the next roundabout on the A414. Follow the underpass into First Avenue/Mandela Avenue. Cross the road and take the narrow path on the right by a signpost to Harlow Museum.

Matching the Villages

A walk between Matching Tye and Matching Green with a church to match.

DISTANCE *3.5 miles (5.7km)*   MINIMUM TIME *1hr 30min*

ASCENT/GRADIENT *Negligible* ▲▲▲   LEVEL OF DIFFICULTY ✦✦✦

PATHS *Bridleways, grass and field-edge paths, 3 stiles*

LANDSCAPE *Ponds, patches of woodland and grassy meadow*

SUGGESTED MAP *OS Explorer 183 Chelmsford & The Rodings, Maldon & Witham*

START / FINISH *Grid reference: TL 515112*

DOG FRIENDLINESS *Notices everywhere warn of grazing stock*

PARKING *Free parking at Matching Tye village hall*

PUBLIC TOILETS *None en route*

You sometimes feel that Essex place names were designed to disorientate and confuse. Either that, or a Saxon cartographer got it all wrong when three tiny villages which form a triangle to the east of Harlow were named Matching Tye, Matching Green and Matching. Matching itself is the oldest of the trio and has changed little since Saxon times when the Maecca or Match people settled in what was then open forest. After the 5th century, this community expanded into Matching Tye and Matching Green.

Take in Two Trails

In this walk we shall discover the flint-and-rubble Church of St Mary the Virgin, built in 1200 over the site of an original Saxon church at Matching. Next to it is the restored Marriage Feast House. A Mr William Chimney built the Feast House in 1480 and allowed local brides and grooms to celebrate their happy day there, a tradition that continued right up until 1936. The large oak tree beside the church was planted to celebrate Queen Victoria's Diamond Jubilee in 1887. These days the Feast House is used as an annexe for church activities. Near by there is a splendid lake filled with waterfowl, a lovely 15th-century timber-framed manor house surrounded by a water-filled moat and a large aisled barn dating back to the 1600s.

Matching Green, to the south-east of Matching, is another village barely touched by time save for a picturesque collection of 18th-century weather-boarded cottages overlooking the green. There used to be shops and half a dozen pubs, but nowadays it is a quiet spot where local people down a pint at the village's only surviving pub, the Chequers. The celebrated portrait artist, Augustus John (1878–1961), whose subjects included Thomas Hardy and George Bernard Shaw, lived in Elm House, next door.

The third village in this trio is Matching Tye renowned for its attractive Conservation Area of historic dwellings clustered round the tiny green. You'll see a range of building materials which include weather-boarding, yellow stock and red brick, red plain clay tiles, slate and thatch. The oldest buildings are the 16th-century Ployters Farm and Little Brewers.

MATTING

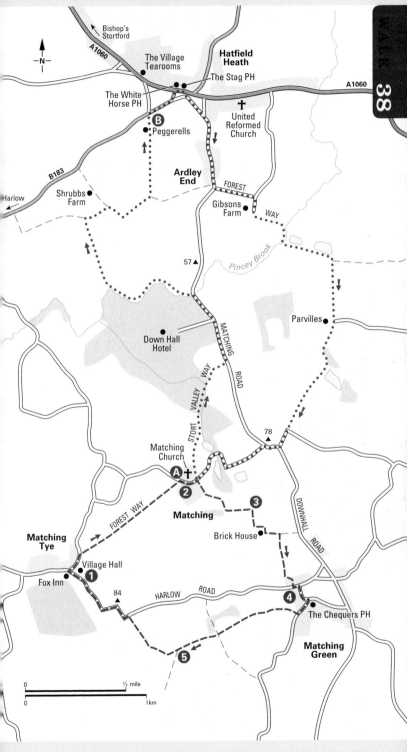

Bishop's Stortford
A1060
The Village Tearooms
Hatfield Heath
The Stag PH
A1060
The White Horse PH
B Peggerells
United Reformed Church
B183
Ardley End
FOREST
Harlow
Shrubbs Farm
Gibsons Farm
WAY
57 ▲
Pincey Brook
Down Hall Hotel
MATCHING
Parvilles
ROAD
STORT VALLEY WAY
78 ▲
Matching Church
A †
2
3
Matching
Brick House
DOWNHALL ROAD
FOREST WAY
Matching Tye
Village Hall
1
Fox Inn
84 ▲
HARLOW ROAD
4
The Chequers PH
5
Matching Green

0 ½ mile
0 1km

WALK 38 DIRECTIONS

1 From Matching Tye village hall turn right. Directly opposite the Fox Inn take the lane, signposted for Sheering and Hatfield Heath. After 200yds (183m), turn right at the fingerpost for the Forest Way and follow the grassy field-edge path, turning right at the end along the bridleway to Matching church.

2 Pass the Marriage Feast House on your left and continue along the road to the right of the church. Take the footpath on your right, opposite the church, through the kissing gate and skirt the moat on your right. After 100yds (91m), cross the stile and walk half left on the cross-field path towards the edge of the line of trees. At the yellow waymark, turn left along the cross-field path.

3 At the mid-field fingerpost, turn right and walk to the line of trees, the boundary of Brick House. Turn left at the fingerpost, keeping the house and paddock on your right. After the paddock turn right across the field towards houses, maintaining direction along the field-edge path. After the playing field on your left, walk between houses into Harlow Road at Matching Green.

4 Turn left and immediately right, then right again, following

the signposts for Ongar and Moreton. After 200yds (183m), turn right at the break in the hedge and go over two stiles in quick succession. Cross the meadow and maintain direction once over the footbridge. Take

the cross-field path towards the line of trees. Keep the trees on your right passing the yellow waymark to cross a footbridge by another copse of trees.

5 Keep ahead and, soon after the footpath appears on your left, bear right on the field-edge path keeping the ditch and trees on your right-hand side. Continue until you reach Harlow Road opposite a house called Roundhouse. Turn left and walk with care along the busy Harlow Road for around 0.5 mile (800m) to return to the village hall at Matching Tye. Here you can finish off with a well-earned rest at the nearby comfortable Fox Inn.

A Hike to Hatfield Heath

A longer loop walk from Matching takes you to Hatfield Heath.

See map and information panel for Walk 38

DISTANCE 6 miles (9.7km) **MINIMUM TIME** 3hrs

ASCENT/GRADIENT 90ft (27m) ▲▲▲ **LEVEL OF DIFFICULTY** ✦✦✦

WALK 39 DIRECTIONS (Walk 38 option)

From Matching you can continue to Hatfield Heath on the Stort Valley Way. Go through the graveyard at Matching church, Point **A**, to the kissing gate. Bear right downhill to cross the footbridge and bear right following the waymark to the stile. Cross the stile, go over a footbridge and turn right along the field-edge path. Turn right over the stile at a fingerpost and then turn left, keeping the stream on your right for 200yds (183m). Cross another stile and keep ahead to bear right over the earth bridge.

Follow the waymark for Stort Valley Way, cross another stile, follow the field-edge path until you turn left on to the Matching road. Pass Down Hall Hotel and turn left on to the waymarked field-edge path, keeping Pincey Brook on your left, for 0.5 mile (800m). Turn right at the fingerpost and before Shrubbs Farm turn right along the permissive path across the field. Cross a footbridge, turn left and continue to Pegerells. Maintain direction until you reach the road via two wooden doors at the sides of houses, Point **B**. Turn right to Hatfield Heath and with your back to The Stag take the tarmac road

to Ardley End. Follow the signpost towards Friars Farm, passing Gibsons Farm and lovely views of rolling countryside. You are now on the Forest Way and should follow these waymarks. Leave Gibsons Farm behind, turn left on to the field-edge path and, at the next waymark, turn right and at the footbridge, turn left.

Climb the steep embankment, pass two reservoirs on your left and turn right uphill to Parvilles, an isolated farmstead.

Bear right on to the grassy path by a Forest Way signpost and head downhill along this bridleway. Soon you see a third reservoir on your left, but maintain direction until you reach Downhall Road. Turn right and follow the sign to Matching church to rejoin Walk 38.

WHERE TO EAT AND DRINK

Two delightful 18th-century pubs, The White Horse and The Stag, can be found at Hatfield Heath. The Stag serves a good range of pub food and is also dog friendly. Dogless walkers may like the offerings at The Village Tearooms nearby.

Hatfield Forest

Walk through part of the once-extensive Royal Forest of Essex.

DISTANCE 4.5 miles (7.2km) **MINIMUM TIME** 2hrs

ASCENT/GRADIENT 89ft (27m) ▲▲▲ **LEVEL OF DIFFICULTY** +++

PATHS Grassy paths and forest trails, 1 stile

LANDSCAPE Ancient coppice woodland, meadows, lakes and marsh

SUGGESTED MAP OS Explorer 195 Braintree & Saffron Walden and 183 Chelmsford & The Rodings

START / FINISH Grid reference: TL 546203

DOG FRIENDLINESS Off-limits around part of lake; but main area dog friendly as long as on lead

PARKING Car parks at main entrance and Shell House inside the forest. Exit gates close at 8pm (free to National Trust members)

PUBLIC TOILETS Beside Forest Café inside forest

WALK 40 DIRECTIONS

In the 12th century Hatfield was under Crown ownership and deer were bred to supply the King's table. Nobody but the King and his cronies were allowed to hunt the hapless peasants, if caught killing animals in the forest they might have their hands cut off, or worse still be executed. By 1446 the forest was owned by a succession of families, including Robert the Bruce, but the last owners from 1729 to 1923 were the Houblons, descendants of the founders of the Bank of England. Today sheep and cattle still graze on the open grassland, barely changed since Norman times, and you might catch a glimpse of shy fallow deer or the smaller Muntjac deer in the coppices.

From the car park follow the surfaced road for 350yds (320m) and at the board walk bear half left across pastureland. After 250yds (229m), go through the wooden gate passing coppiced hornbeam woods to the lake on your right. Bear right for 70yds (64m), to cross the dam dividing the lake, home to many birds throughout the year, and follow the path to Shell House.

Shell House was built by the Houblons who lived at Hallingbury Place to the west of the forest, and created the lake in about 1746 by damming Shermore Brook. They bred peacocks, planted exotic trees and held grand lakeside picnics. In 1923 they sold the forest and

WHERE TO EAT AND DRINK

The refurbished Forest Café inside the forest offers tasty snacks and drinks, which you can enjoy at the picnic tables beside the lake. Not as grand as Houblon lakeside affairs, it's pleasant enough and the only peacock is a decorative one above the Shell House door.

HATFIELD FOREST

London Road, where stage coaches from East Anglia would cross the bridge over Shermore Brook. Keeping close to the woods on your left, continue north-westwards for 0.5 mile (800m), until you meet a cross path. Go through a gate and turn right here, on to the Flitch Way.

The railway track, a casualty of Dr Beeching's cuts in 1969, formed part of the line linking Bishops Stortford and Braintree. Now the Flitch Way, this path buzzes with butterflies and birds in summer while slow worms, grass snakes and lizards make their homes on the south-facing banks. After 300yds (274m) look out for where a stream runs under the footpath, turn right down the steep embankment and continue with the brook on your left.

Keep ahead along the edge of the meadow, passing to the right of a pond and into woodland. Cross a footbridge and a stile and continue straight ahead on to the widest path to the next cross path and turn right along the path between

for a while its future remained uncertain, especially when the new owner happened to be a timber merchant. Then naturalist Edward North Buxton came to the rescue writing out a cheque as part payment for the forest before he died. His sons completed the transaction and gave the forest to the National Trust.

Go through the car park at Shell House and follow the path south, with the smaller lake on your left, to the wide grassy path until you reach a 'wantz', an Essex word for a junction where rides intersect. You are now at Collins Coppice. Turn right here, on to the wide grassy bridleway for 250yds (229m) and bear right on to the plain, keeping Forest Lodge on your left-hand side. Continue north on the wide plain to join a gravel track and passing Warren Cottage on your right.

Warren Cottage used to house the warrener, who in medieval times would look after the rabbit warren. Rabbits were introduced from Spain in the 12th century for food and fur. The remains of the warren are still visible in the form of pillow-shaped mounds behind the cottage.

Bear left across the wide grassy plain dotted with maple, ash and hawthorn. This was the former

the last of the coppiced trees, before emerging on to open grass land. Bear slightly right keeping trees of Elgin Coppice to your right. Cross the tarmac road and maintain direction back to the car park resplendent with the ancient pollarded trees which welcomed you at the beginning of the walk.

Pretty Ugley

*An easy ramble taking in views of undulating countryside
and part of the Harcamlow Way.*

DISTANCE 5.5 miles (8.8km)   MINIMUM TIME 2hrs 15min

ASCENT/GRADIENT 75ft (23m) ▲▲▲   LEVEL OF DIFFICULTY +++

PATHS Woodland and grassy tracks, field-edge, some road walking,
2 stiles (but likely to be removed)

LANDSCAPE Gently undulating arable and grazing farmland,
some woodland and isolated farmsteads

SUGGESTED MAP OS Explorer 195 Braintree & Saffron Walden

START / FINISH Grid reference: TL 513288

DOG FRIENDLINESS Decent-sized field-edge paths but on lead through farms

PARKING Car park at The Chequers pub, Cambridge Road

PUBLIC TOILETS None en route

Ugley village, straddling the busy Cambridge to London road and a
few miles north of Stansted Mountfitchet, is the butt of many jokes.
It's tempting not to start this walk without references to ugly people, ugly
ducklings and ugly sisters, such descriptions of course being in the eye of
the beholder. But it is nothing like the Cinderella of Essex villages and is,
in fact, a pretty hamlet consisting of delightful houses, a pub, village hall,
church and even an Ugley Womens Institute, although no members have
yet entered the Ugley Beauty Competition! Walkers, on the other hand,
will discover just one blot on the landscape and that is the black netting
of the landfill site, visible for miles around, on this otherwise lovely walk
through gently undulating countryside.

A Ghostly Tale

The village is named after Ugga the Viking who set up home in a clearing, or
ley, in what was once a huge forest. Those forests have long since gone and
today are replaced by arable farmland, patches of woodland, plantations of
pine forests, isolated farmsteads and the tiny hamlets of Ugley and Ugley
Green. Ghost stories are rife in Ugley and where better a place to start
a spooky trail than from the Chequers pub. This 16th-century coaching
inn stands near the site of a Viking burial ground and was almost in ruins
when its present owner bought it some years ago. It's said that some parts
of the pub are haunted and that if you linger long enough you can feel an
inexplicably chilly draft. If you're extra vigilant you may see the ghost-like
figure of a wizened Victorian lady dressed from head to toe in black. Some
tradesmen swear they will not work in the pub unless there are plenty of
people around.

From the pub we walk into the woods, now pine plantations, where
Ugga and his friends may have set up camp, and continue on to the
Harcamlow Way, part of a figure-of-eight 140 mile (225km) cross country
route between Harlow and Cambridge. On the way you pass the dilapidated

UGLEY

farmstead of Wade's Hall, with its outbuildings entwined in ivy and just the sort of place to spot Ugga's ghost. Bollington Hall, the next farmhouse, stands majestically on a hill overlooking gently undulating farmland and it is indeed a pleasure to walk along this landowner's wide field-edge paths with wonderful views of Ugley.

Our walk continues to Ugley Green where The Place, a magnificent thatched house, overlooks the green. A few miles across open fields brings us to Ugley Church where the Victorian lady in black sometimes hovers amid the gravestones. Hurry on to the Chequers for some sustenance, but make sure you avoid sitting in that chilly draft…

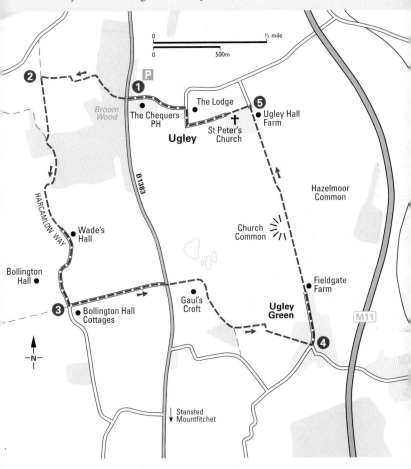

WALK 41 DIRECTIONS

❶ Cross the B1383 with care and follow the fingerpost directly opposite The Chequers through Broom Wood. Cross the stile and follow the yellow waymarks through the plantation of conifers, via the plank bridge and another stile. After the stile, turn left and follow the field-edge path to the right. Maintain direction following the field-edge path right and left until you reach the cross path.

❷ Turn left on to the wide cross-field path towards conifers. Go through the gap in the hedgerow

WALK 41

The lack of choice of eateries in the area is compensated by the variety of food at The Chequers pub in Cambridge Road, Ugley. This former 16th-century coaching inn has plenty of character, welcomes walkers and cyclists and has a garden where you can relax with your dog. Choose from an extensive carnivorous and vegetarian menu or opt for tasty sandwiches or salads.

and left on the wide bridle path, which is the Harcamlow Way. Ignore the path left and bear right to continue along the Harcamlow Way south, with fields on your right and the conifer wood to your left. Maintain your direction passing the farm buildings of Wade's Hall, followed by the isolated farmstead of Bollington Hall. From now on the path is tarmac, with arable fields on either side and clear views of the houses at Ugley.

❸ Turn left in front of Bollington Hall Cottages and take the straight road towards the B1383, with the skyline of Ugley looming ahead. Cross the road with care and follow the narrow, overgrown path ahead through Gaul's Croft. This well-defined path meanders through the small thick forest bounded by bramble. At the next waymark, keep ahead along the field-edge path and after crossing an earth bridge turn right, and

then left by a waymark to emerge at peaceful Ugley Green. Stop for a breather here to take in the architecture of elegant houses from various periods, some of which are thatched.

❹ Turn left along the tarmac road following the 'Fieldgate Lane no-through road' sign. Maintain direction past houses, passing the smart Fieldgate Farm on your right. The road becomes a wide muddy track bisecting arable fields and eventually reaches the outbuildings of Ugley Hall Farm where you maintain direction and go through a metal gate to join a road.

Look for the 32nd milestone from London on the Cambridge Road, famous among cycling enthusiasts of all ages. It is just north of the Chequers pub and is the start and finishing point of many cycling trials. You may see members of the 32nd Association (or their ghosts!) formed from various clubs throughout Essex who make regular use of this road.

❺ At the public footpath sign just before the cottages on the right, turn left and go through a wooden gate and walk through the churchyard of St Peter's Church. Keep ahead and follow the tarmac road through grazing fields, passing The Lodge, where you turn left and return via Patmore End to the car park.

Ugley Green has a clutch of beautiful thatched houses overlooking the green. If you cross the green and walk towards the bus stop you will see a perfectly preserved water pump beside a huge pudding stone. Pudding stones are glacial deposits dating back 180 million years and look like a boiled suet pudding studded with cherries and currants. Pilgrims would use them as medieval markers in much the same way as we use fingerposts and road signs.

Taking Off from Stansted

A rural walk beside the runway of London's third international airport and a plane-spotter's paradise.

DISTANCE 3.25 miles (5.3km)   **MINIMUM TIME** 1hr 30min

ASCENT/GRADIENT 54ft (16m) ▲▲▲   **LEVEL OF DIFFICULTY** ✦✦✦

PATHS Grass and gravel tracks, grassy verge, field-edge and some road walking

LANDSCAPE Arable farmland, open meadow, airport runway and airport installations

SUGGESTED MAP OS Explorer 195 Braintree & Saffron Walden

START / FINISH Grid reference: TL 528239

DOG FRIENDLINESS Grassy verge next to airport perimeter fence is a great place for an off-lead sniff

PARKING Informal street parking at Burton End village

PUBLIC TOILETS None en route

Stansted Airport is London's third international airport. Built on the site of an American airbase, its construction ended 50 years of debate as to where it should be sited. During the 1930s plans were announced for building an airport at Fairlop, near Hainault Forest, but these were overtaken by shortlists drawn up between the 1960s and 1970s for sites much further away from the urban fringe. One of these was Stansted and, after prolonged public debate, the airport opened in 1991.

One of the conditions of construction was that no soil was to be taken from the site, and as a result some interesting archaeological finds from neolithic to medieval times were discovered, some of which are displayed at Saffron Walden Museum. The striking design of the airport terminal, by Sir Norman Foster and much admired by visitors, is an example of how closely rural Essex is tied to the fortunes and changing needs of London.

The airport is one of the biggest employers in the area, currently employing 12,000, and is one of the fastest growing in England with modern terminal facilities. These include a spacious one-level terminal with natural light, minimum walking distances for passengers and state of the art equipment to monitor noise levels.

Going for a Burton

This walk starts at the tiny hamlet of Burton End, which is the nearest you'll get to the runway to see aircraft taking off and landing. Burton End with its attractive 18th- and 19th-century cottages and houses, like its neighbour, Tye Green with its pleasant green and thatched dwellings, seems untouched by the development of the airport and their proximity to the busy M11. As you traverse arable fields you can't fail to hear the roar of aircraft engines as they take off or come into land. In your meander across the beautiful rolling countryside of north-west Essex you may be surprised to discover a railway track, a spur line from Stansted Mountfitchet, which disappears beneath the airport runway. This line is the Stansted Express, which connects passengers with London's Liverpool Street Station and the airport terminal.

By far the most frequent visitors to the quiet lanes of Burton End and Tye Green are plane-spotters who come out in all weathers to pursue their hobby from the grassy verges skirting the airport perimeter fence. If you're into plane-spotting, or just enjoy the countryside with rather surreal views of roaring metal-winged birds, rather than the feathered kind that twitters and sings in woodland, then this walk may be right up your runway.

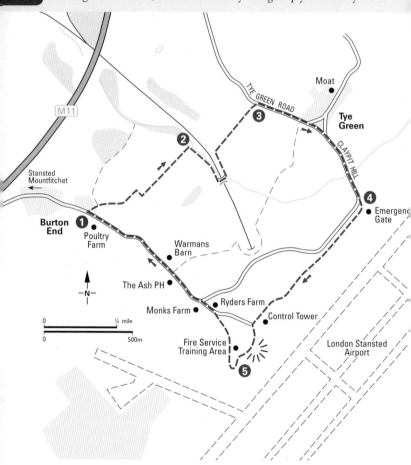

WALK 42 DIRECTIONS

❶ Follow the public footpath sign beside a restored water pump at Burton End and walk between houses to the arable field. Ignore the waymarked fingerpost and follow the field-edge path with the ditch and hedgerows to your right. At the waymark, cross between bushes and maintain

direction with the ditch and hedgerow on your left. Maintain direction, turning right and left at the waymarks, and go over a plank footbridge until you reach the waymark on the edge of the copse of trees.

❷ Turn right and after 300yds (274m) go over a stile and cross the railway cutting. This is the spur line to Stansted Airport so you can even plane and train spot at the same time. Once over a second stile, turn left with the railway on your left along the left-hand field edge for 50yds (46m). At the next waymark, turn right on to the cross-field path to emerge at Tye Green Road.

❸ Turn right on to Tye Green Road. At the houses, turn left to explore old cottages and the

moated farm at Tye Green. Follow the track around The Green back to Tye Green Road and turn left along the road which changes its name to Claypit Hill. The road bears sharply right, opposite is the emergency gateway set in the perimeter fence of Stansted Airport. From here, if there is room, you can jostle for position with plane-spotters to watch aircraft landing.

❹ In front of the fence, turn right to walk along the verge between the airport perimeter fence and the road. Maintain your direction following the path around the control tower and fire service training centre.

❺ Turn right on to the farm track between Ryders Farm and Monks Farm to the three-way junction at Belmer Road and then turn left. Call in at The Ash public house on your left, although the tree after which it is named no longer exists. Here there is a large car park and garden area, popular at lunch time with aircraft maintenance workers from the nearby hangars. From the pub, turn left passing Warmans Barn on your right and return to your car at Burton End.

On the Ground at Stansted

A suprisingly rural saunter around the ancient and modern sights of Stansted Mountfitchet.

DISTANCE 5.75 miles (9.2km)   **MINIMUM TIME** 2hrs 15min

ASCENT/GRADIENT 101ft (34m) ▲▲▲   **LEVEL OF DIFFICULTY** ✦✦✦

PATHS Grassy and forest tracks, field-edge and some street walking

LANDSCAPE Arable farmland, grazing meadow, some forest

SUGGESTED MAP OS Explorer 195 Braintree & Saffron Walden

START / FINISH Grid reference: TL 515248

DOG FRIENDLINESS On lead for most of way

PARKING Pay-and-display at Lower Street

PUBLIC TOILETS Lower Street car park

Some passengers flying in from the Continent bound for Stansted may be surprised to peer out of the window and spot a Norman castle on a hill, around which is a village, a brook and a railway line. On landing they may be even more surprised to learn that this castle is only 2 miles (3.2km) away at Stansted Mountfitchet. In this walk we take a trip back in time to the 11th century and explore the rural delights surrounding Stansted Montfichet.

Stansted appears in the Domesday Book as Stansteda, a Saxon name meaning stony place. After the Norman conquest, William I granted the lordship of the manor to the Gernon family, who later changed their name to Montfichet. The Montfichet family came from Normandy and during the 12th century Richard de Montfichet built a motte-and-bailey castle. The second Richard de Montfichet was one of five Essex barons who forced King John to sign the Magna Carta, and in revenge the King destroyed the castle in 1215. All that remains are the mound and part of the stone wall, but today you can visit an imaginative reconstruction of the castle complete with Norman village and interpretative displays showing what life was like in Norman times.

This walk takes in the pretty windmill on a hill at the back of the village before cutting across Stansted Brook and the railway line to old Stansted. We take a pleasant footpath passing the Manor House, one of the original vicarages of the beautiful Norman church, St Mary the Virgin, that stands in the grounds of Stansted Hall. The church, another legacy of the Montfichet family, contains the worn figure of a 14th-century cross-legged knight believed to be Richard de Montfichet. Stansted Hall is now the Arthur Findlay College for Psychic Studies, colloquially known as 'Spook Hall'.

You will also pass through the delightful hamlet of Birchanger which is blessed with views of rolling countryside and woodlands. In Stansted Mountfitchet you can see old houses and pubs, some dating back to the 16th and 17th centuries and the village sign, depicting the Montfichet shield, standing as a statement reminding visitors and locals that their heritage must be conserved.

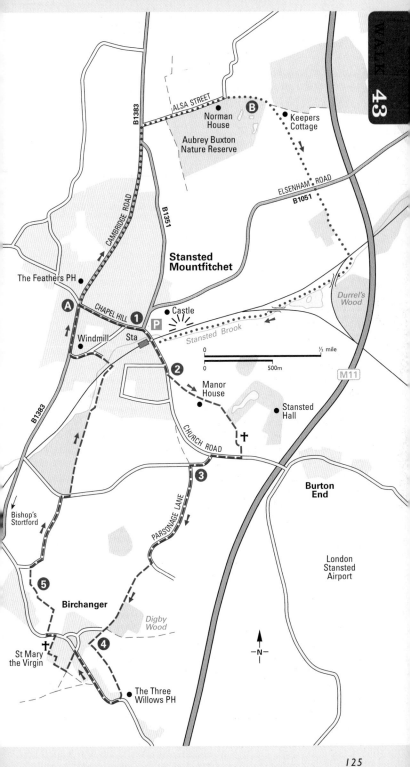

ALSA STREET

B1383

Norman House

B

Keepers Cottage

Aubrey Buxton Nature Reserve

ELSENHAM ROAD

B1051

CAMBRIDGE ROAD

B1351

Stansted Mountfitchet

The Feathers PH

Durrel's Wood

A

CHAPEL HILL

1

P

● Castle

Stansted Brook

◄

Windmill

Sta

2

0   ½ mile

0   500m

Manor House

Stansted Hall

✝

M11

B1383

CHURCH ROAD

3

Burton End

Bishop's Stortford

PARSONAGE LANE

London Stansted Airport

5

Birchanger

Digby Wood

St Mary the Virgin ✝

4

─N─

The Three Willows PH

WALK 43 DIRECTIONS

W A L K 43

❶ From the car park turn left into Church Road, cross the railway bridge and, a few paces after Churchfields, bear left on to the concrete track by a public footpath sign.

❷ Maintain direction along the track keeping to the left of Manor House where it becomes a narrow path. Pass by the line of trees and an arable field to your left. Keep the church to your left and follow the path to Church Road. Turn right and then left into Forest Hall Road past the leisure centre.

❸ Turn left along Parsonage Lane and after the farm buildings on your left, turn right across a field heading towards a public bridleway signpost. Pass to the right of Digby Wood towards houses and where the wood ends keep ahead and look out for a grey scout hut on the left.

❹ Turn left at the scout hut and right along an enclosed path by a public footpath sign, to reach The Three Willows pub. Turn right along Birchanger Lane and turn left at a public footpath sign beside Gower Barn. At the next waymark post turn right and follow waymarks to the church on your left. Cross Birchanger Lane with care, bear left and turn right to join a footpath past allotments.

Go through a copse bearing right to cross a plank footbridge. At the field-edge turn left and look out for a set of steps on your left.

❺ Turn right across the field passing to the right of a metal barrier to join Tot Lane by a public footpath sign. Turn right and at the top, turn right again and then left along an enclosed footpath just before a new housing estate. At the end, join West Road, turn left to cross the green footbridge over the railway line and catch a glimpse of the windmill. At the bottom of the slope turn left and cross the footbridge over the brook on your right. Turn left along Brook Road and right into Millside passing the windmill. Turn right and at the cross-roads turn right again and continue down Chapel Hill to the car park.

Stansted Mountfitchet

*A different loop takes in wild places by a railway,
nature reserve and castle.*

See map and information panel for Walk 43

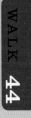

WALK 44

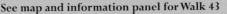

DISTANCE 4.75 miles (7.7km)	MINIMUM TIME 2hrs
ASCENT/GRADIENT 105ft (32m) ▲▲▲	LEVEL OF DIFFICULTY +++

WALK 44 DIRECTIONS
(Walk 43 option)

At the crossroads on Chapel Hill, Point **A**, turn right into the Cambridge Road, an old Roman road, now the B1383, where a Victorian drinking fountain stands on the former site of the Cock Beer house. The Cambridge Road used to be the old turnpike road along which there were several coaching inns. One of these, The Feathers on the left, dates back to the mid-19th century and is adjacent to some fine examples of 17th- and 18th- century pargetted and thatched buildings, evidence of a much older village which existed long before the airport.

After 1 mile (1.6km), turn right into Alsa Street passing the converted barns, which form the Alsa Business Park on your right. This is followed by the high wall of the imposing 18th-century Norman House. As the road bears sharp left, go straight ahead on to the bridleway and after 100yds (91m) you reach the entrance to the Aubrey Buxton Nature Reserve, Point **B**, on your right. Originally the pleasure park to Norman House, this lovely woodland with six ponds was donated by Lady Buxton in 1976, and is managed by the Essex Wildlife Trust.

Keep ahead to pass to the right of Keepers Cottage. Turn right at the Y-junction of paths and follow the bridleway downhill to Elsenham Road. Cross the road with care.

Follow the footpath opposite farm buildings downhill and into a tunnel under the London-to-Cambridge railway. Although surrounded by a triangle of road and rail bustle, formed by two railtracks and a motorway, this area is full of wildlife provided by the juxtaposition of Durrell's Wood and Stansted Brook. Turn right and pass through another tunnel, turn right over a footbridge and then turn left and maintain direction with the railway on your right and Stansted Brook on your left.

The path here may be narrow and very muddy after heavy rain. But you are surrounded by thick gorse, baby oak, reeds, sedges and the ubiquitous thistle which provide a wonderful habitat for all manner of insects. Pass through another tunnel and at the end of the footpath metal steps ascend beside a white timbered house to the bridge on Church Road. Turn right for views of the castle and rejoin Walk 43.

A Roam Around Roding Valley Nature Reserve

A wildlife wander on the former site of RAF Chigwell.

DISTANCE *3 miles (4.8km)* **MINIMUM TIME** *1hr 15min*

ASCENT/GRADIENT *Negligible* ▲▲▲ **LEVEL OF DIFFICULTY** ✚✚✚

PATHS *Wide byways, tracks and riverside footpaths*

LANDSCAPE *River bank, open meadows and some urban views*

SUGGESTED MAP *OS Explorer 174 Epping Forest & Lee Valley*

START / FINISH *Grid reference: TQ 430943*

DOG FRIENDLINESS *Positively dog friendly, no stiles and off lead*

PARKING *Small free car park by David Lloyd Club off Roding Lane*

PUBLIC TOILETS *None en route*

WALK 45 DIRECTIONS

Roding Valley Meadows Nature Reserve covers approximately 158 acres (64ha) and is situated on traditionally managed hay meadows which, from 1938 to 1968, were occupied by RAF Chigwell. Over 3,000 people lived and worked here in more than 100 buildings, which included hangars, a theatre, a post office and a shop. Now demolished, it's hard to believe that this nature reserve with its peaceful paths and meadows was once home to such a community.

From the information board at the entrance by the kissing gate there are two paths. The one straight ahead is wide and gravelly, but to start the walk take the path on the right and up the steps of the steep embankment. This narrow hillside was created from earth dug out during the construction of the M11 but is seldom used and has become an excellent hunting ground for kestrels and sparrow hawks. Much of the original site of the RAF base now lies beneath the

motorway. Also from here you can look down on the recreation area and the lake which, although not part of the reserve, is a popular spot for many waterfowl. After exploring this area return to your starting point and take the main path through the kissing gate into the reserve.

Follow the path through the reserve and, ignoring paths branching off to the right and left, keep ahead passing oak and hornbeam. The concrete area you will pass marks the site of RAF Chigwell. Continue along the concrete track until you reach a grassy roundabout surrounded by open meadow. The seating here provides a good picnic area and a place to watch for skylarks nesting in the meadow ahead.

Now take the narrow path which leads away from the concrete roundabout and go through a kissing gate beside a sign, 'footpath number 8'. Continue along an enclosed path beside Four Acres Field to the left. Continue along the cross path, an ancient green lane which once formed part of the drovers' and packhorse route from Epping Forest to Romford market. This green lane contains an incredible variety of trees and shrubs including ash, oak, elder, elm, blackthorn, dogwood, hombeam, crab apple and hazel. You might also see plants such as honeysuckle, bluebell and foxglove. Turn right and continue along this path towards the tall thin chimney which is a Victorian vent for underground sewers. Bear left into the large grass area known as Lower Mead following the waymark. This area is cut regularly for hay which, combined with winter grazing, is a traditional method of looking after grassland and encourages wild flowers to grow. In spring it is a riot of colour and the hedgerows nearby are a section of almost 10 miles (16.1km) of hedgerow that is managed by laying and coppicing.

The path now continues with the River Roding to your right providing a habitat for kingfishers, dragonflies, damselflies, bream and sticklebacks. After 300yds (274m), cross the river on Charlie Moule's footbridge, built in the 1950s to replace stepping stones. Turn left after the footbridge along a concrete path with the river on your left. Follow this

WALK 45

meandering path beside the river bank, crossing a small wooden footbridge. Later the path veers away from the river and ahead, through the trees, you will see a lake. This is a good place to watch wildfowl such as Canada geese, mallard ducks, moorhens and coots. The lake was dug to provide the nearby M11 with gravel.

Keep ahead, passing a cricket pavilion to cross White Bridge over the River Roding, and re-enter the nature reserve. Turn left in the direction of the red waymark and go through a kissing-gate later bearing away from the river and lake to join a gravel path. Turn right and retrace your steps back to the start of the walk.

WHAT TO LOOK OUT FOR

Near the picnic area, by the grassy roundabout, look for the thick iron rings in the ground from which barrage balloons from RAF Chigwell were strung during World War Two. Just before you reach this roundabout, on the left by some trees, is a flat stone, with an inscription by an airman from the unit, which reads, '1943 Intone'. This commemorates an operation involving a Mobile Signals Unit from RAF Chigwell, which went to the Azores to destroy German submarines.

Epping Forest Retreat

*Follow Queen Victoria's path to the opening
of the forest to Londoners.*

DISTANCE 7.25 miles (11.7km)   **MINIMUM TIME** 3hrs 30min

ASCENT/GRADIENT 227ft (70m) ▲▲▲   **LEVEL OF DIFFICULTY** ✦✦✦

PATHS Woodland paths and bridleways, some road

LANDSCAPE Ponds, ancient woodland and open heathland

SUGGESTED MAP OS Explorer 174 Epping Forest & Lee Valley

START / FINISH Grid reference: TQ 404950

DOG FRIENDLINESS Great fun, though a bit muddy.
Keep on lead around horses

PARKING Free car park on A1069 at Connaught Water

PUBLIC TOILETS Epping Forest Conservation Centre

Shaped like a crescent and extending 12 miles (19.3km) south from Epping to Wanstead Flats, Epping Forest is divided by the Epping New Road which gives access from north-east London to the M25. But for all the traffic, you need step back only a little to discover tranquil tracks and pathways meandering through 6,000 acres (2,430ha) of ancient woodland. For Epping Forest is one of the few places where you can still see the effects of medieval forest management and is a popular recreational retreat.

A Gift from a Queen

You can follow Queen Victoria's route from Connaught Water, near Chingford Station where she arrived in 1882 to declare, 'It gives me the greatest satisfaction to dedicate this beautiful forest to the use and enjoyment of my people for all time'. She rode in an open carriage along Fairmead Bottom to High Beach to the cheers of the crowds of Cockneys.

Prior to this, the forest was a hunting ground reserved for royals. Queen Elizabeth I used to hunt from the lodge named after her, now the Epping Forest Museum, and probably galloped over an early Roman settlement, Loughton Camp, a few miles to the east. Stray off pathways and into deep shaded glades and you might spot fallow or muntjac deer, descendants of the dark fallow deer introduced by James I in 1612. You can also enjoy the landscape near the Kings Oak pub where Henry VIII breakfasted on 19 May, 1536 as he waited to hear that Anne Boleyn had been executed.

At the Epping Forest Conservation Centre, a trail leads you through an ancient landscape of coppiced and pollarded trees. In medieval times cattle and deer were free to graze and woodsmen harvested wood for domestic purposes, a practice which ceased in 1878. Trees were coppiced, or cut to ground level, allowing new shoots to grow from the stump, but if left unfenced made easy fodder for animals. To save the trees from further damage the branches were cut above head height every 12 to 15 years, a system known as pollarding. Explore the forest today and you'll find several thousand of these pollarded trees, identifiable by their massive crowns.

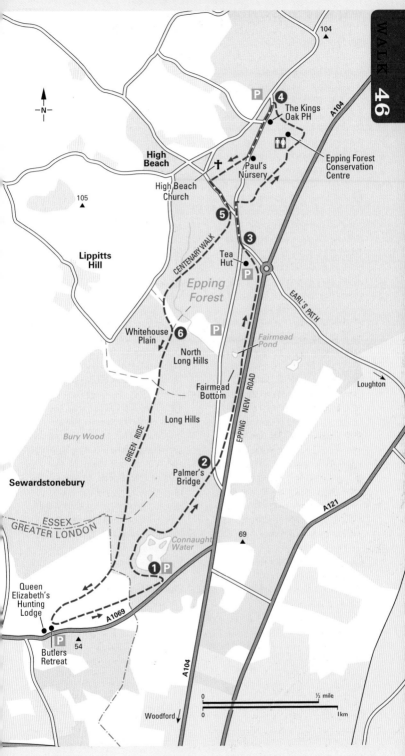

104 ▲

P

4 The Kings Oak PH

A104

Epping Forest Conservation Centre

High Beach

† Paul's Nursery

High Beach Church

105 ▲

5

Lippitts Hill

CENTENARY WALK

Epping Forest

3

Tea Hut

P

EARL'S PATH

Whitehouse Plain 6

P

Fairmead Pond

North Long Hills

Loughton

Fairmead Bottom

EPPING NEW ROAD

Long Hills

Bury Wood

GREEN RIDE

Sewardstonebury

2 Palmer's Bridge

A121

ESSEX
GREATER LONDON

Connaught Water

69 ▲

1 P

Queen Elizabeth's Hunting Lodge

A1069

Butlers Retreat

P 54 ▲

A104

0   ½ mile
0   1 km

Woodford

WALK 46 DIRECTIONS

1 From the car park walk between wooden posts and bear left on the gravel path which hugs Connaught Water. Walk around the lake for 800yds (732m), turn left over the footbridge and along the path with high trees towards Fairmead Bottom. This low-lying area may flood after rain.

2 After 400yds (366m), turn left on to the disused tarmac road and after a few paces cross Palmer's Bridge and bear right on to the grassy track, which continues ahead close to the A104 on your right. The path crosses meadows to Fairmead Pond on your left and after 750yds (686m), turn left on to the road uphill and into the car park where there is a tea hut.

3 Continue up the tarmac road for 100yds (91m) and turn right by the metal gate on to the wide hoggin bridleway, which undulates through high woods and pollarded beech trees. Maintain direction for 0.5 mile (800m) and at a crossing of paths take the path left, which leads into the wooden fenced enclosure of Epping Forest Conservation Centre.

4 Leave the Conservation Centre by the front path, turn left and walk past The Kings Oak public house. After 300yds

(274m), with Paul's Nursery on your left, take the path right. Walk under high trees for 250yds (229m) to reach the tarmac road and the secluded location of High Beech church. With the church behind you, turn left downhill and after 300yds (274m), turn right on to the path between high pollarded trees.

5 This is the Centenary Walk, which maintains direction through thick woodland for 0.5 mile (800m) to the deep cutting of the small brook. Walk downhill south-west, keeping the brook on your right and after 400yds (366m), at the wide grassy cross path, go left.

6 After 300yds (274m), turn right on to the Green Ride bridleway. This popular horse ride bisects North Long Hills and Whitehouse Plain. At the confluence of paths maintain your direction through Bury Wood and at a crossing of paths take the next path on the right which leads to open heathland. Take the path half right and ahead notice the wooden frame of Butlers Retreat, a popular watering hole next to Queen Elizabeth's Hunting Lodge. Turn left downhill by the A1069 and return to the car park.

A Scout Round Gilwell Park

A fairly challenging walk combining superb London views and the wooded parkland of the headquarters of the Scout Association.

DISTANCE 6 miles (9.7km)   **MINIMUM TIME** 2hrs 30min

ASCENT/GRADIENT 231ft (70m) ▲▲▲   **LEVEL OF DIFFICULTY** +++

PATHS Grassy paths, forest tracks, green lanes, some stretches of road, several stiles

LANDSCAPE Forest, park, reservoir, waterways and rolling countryside

SUGGESTED MAP OS Explorer 174 Epping Forest & Lee Valley

START / FINISH Grid reference: TQ 387963

DOG FRIENDLINESS Great open spaces and forest to sniff about in, but watch for horses and packs of cub scouts

PARKING Free car park in Gilwell Lane

PUBLIC TOILETS None en route

Every scout has heard of Gilwell Park, the international training and camp centre for the Scout Association. Set on a plateau and flanked by King George's Reservoir in the west and Epping Forest in the east, the 108 acre (43.7ha) wooded estate was bought for the Scout Association in 1919 by a wealthy Scottish publisher, William F de Bois Maclaren.

Through the Estate

A public footpath passes through the estate giving views of the monuments, statues, camp fire circles, scout huts and in the distance, the White House, now Gilwell Park Hotel and Conference Centre, before descending towards the reservoir. The White House dates back to the 15th century but was nothing like the grand building you see today. In the mid-18th century it was rebuilt and over the years extended, and renamed, by various owners.

Perhaps the most dynamic occupants were William and Margaret Chinnery, who lived here from 1792 to 1812 and brought new life to the area. They were patrons of the arts, threw lavish parties and were seen in all the right places. But tragedy struck; two of their children died, one aged 12 and the other 21, and shortly afterwards William was dismissed from his Civil Service post when he was accused of fraud. He fled to Gothenburg and never returned and Margaret moved to Paris.

Scouting for Boys

In 1858 William Alfred Gibbs, better known as the inventor of Gibbs Dentifrice toothpaste, became the new owner but he couldn't afford the upkeep of the house, which was in ruins by the time it was sold to the Scout Association for £7,000. In 1994 the White House was completely renovated but if you visit today take care; they say that some parts are haunted and that a female ghost walks late at night lamenting the loss of her children. Some have heard strange rattling chains and clanking footsteps and others swear they have spotted the figure of Dick Turpin astride Black Bess.

GILWELL PARK

Scouting round Gilwell Park involves some sharp climbs and slippery descents especially after rain, but the views of north London from the top of Barn Hill are well worth the effort. This walk also takes in the forest paths around Lippitts Hill where you may hear close range gunfire and helicopters hovering above a set of army-like buildings. You could be forgiven for thinking that you have accidentally strayed in to an SAS training camp but the truth is that you are adjacent to the firearms training camp and helicopter base of the Metropolitan Police. Lord Baden-Powell of Gilwell, founder of the Scout Movement, no doubt would have warned his protégés to watch out and, if anything, to 'Be Prepared.'

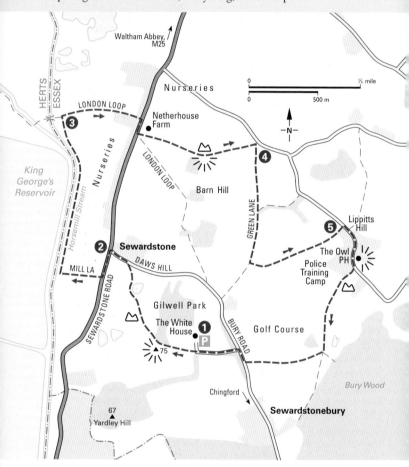

WALK 47 DIRECTIONS

❶ From the Wilson Way visitor car park pass to the left of The White House and turn right to pass through the gates of Gilwell Park following the yellow waymark. Keep to the wide grassy path between trees and the Scout Association buildings. At the top of the hill there are panoramic views of the reservoir. Follow the steep downhill path with the wood and the pond on your right and go through a squeezer stile to emerge beside the village hall at Sewardstone.

GILWELL PARK

2 Turn left into Dawes Hill and left again into Sewardstone Road. Turn right into Mill Lane passing houses and maintain your direction on the downhill track towards King George's Reservoir. Turn right and follow the track, with the reservoir and Horsemill Stream on your left, to the footbridge over the stream.

3 Do not cross the bridge. Go straight through the gate and turn right on to the waymarked London Loop path, walking east until you reach Sewardstone Road. Turn right and after 100yds (91m), turn left over the stile and ignore the London Loop path right. Walk up the steep north flank of Barn Hill, stopping to look around occasionally at tremendous views over reservoirs, Epping Forest and Waltham Abbey.

4 After crossing the gravel path and a stile opposite this, turn right on to the wide Green Lane. Maintain direction and turn left at the second public footpath signpost marked 'Lippitts Hill'. Follow the yellow waymark posts across the golf course, later bearing left past the police firearms training camp fence on your right and don't be alarmed if it sounds as though there's a war going on. The marksmen are well away from you.

WHILE YOU'RE THERE

Depending on the weather and availability of staff you may be able to join a guided tour of Gilwell Park, which includes the campsite, the White House and the training centre. Visitors should report to the Warden in Camp Square or telephone 0208 498 5300 in advance. You can also buy a range of booklets, souvenirs and maps from the shop on the site.

5 At Lippitts Hill, turn right passing the training camp and The Owl pub, the gardens of which afford lovely views across Epping Forest. Fifty yards (46m) after the pub turn right at the public footpath signpost, go up wooden steps and on to the steep downhill path via steps. Maintain your direction between horse paddocks and cross the wooden footbridge and another stile. Follow the path over undulating meadow across the flank of the hill, then downhill to houses on your left. At the public footpath sign to Sewardstonebury go through the metal gate and follow the line of oak trees across West Essex Golf Course. Maintain direction across fairways and past houses to emerge via a stile into Bury Road. Turn right and then first left to return to the car park.

WHAT TO LOOK OUT FOR

Big Mac, nothing to do with a hamburger, is a clock tower in Camp Square named after camp warden, Alfred Macintosh, who advocated that a clock should be placed high enough so that it could be seen right across the main camping field of Gilwell Park. Scouts from Bermondsey raised the cash for Big Mac, which is visible from the footpath at the start of the walk.

WHERE TO EAT AND DRINK

The 18th-century White House is a conference and training centre for the Scout Association but doubles as a hotel with a pleasant restaurant. Combine lunch with an informal tour of the public rooms, decorated with scouting memorabilia and paintings, including one used on the set of ITV's *Coronation Street*. Pub grub can be had at The Owl at Lippitts Hill opposite the police firearms training camp.

Overleaf: The parish church and abbey ruins at Waltham Abbey (Walk 48 / 49)

Lee Valley Park

*An adventurous and challenging walk following
the 'gunpowder plot' at Waltham Abbey, waterways,
ancient woodlands and a host of views.*

WALK 48

DISTANCE 7.5 miles (12.1km)	**MINIMUM TIME** 4hrs

ASCENT/GRADIENT 269ft (82m) ▲▲▲ **LEVEL OF DIFFICULTY** +++

PATHS Grassy riverside, steep field paths, green lanes prone to mud after rain, short stretch of road, 5 stiles

LANDSCAPE Country park, woodland, waterways and marshes

SUGGESTED MAP OS Explorer 174 Epping Forest & Lee Valley

START / FINISH Grid reference: TL 384015

DOG FRIENDLINESS A lot of time on lead. Waltham Road unpleasant

PARKING Free car park at Cornmill Meadows, closes at 6pm

PUBLIC TOILETS Near the Bittern Watchpoint at Fishers Green

You could spend an entire day doing nothing more strenuous than enjoying the recreational facilities of the Lee Valley Country Park. The 1,000 acres (405ha) on either side of the River Lee between Waltham Abbey in Essex and Broxbourne in Hertfordshire consist of lakes, waterways, open space and countryside linked by paths, walkways and cycle tracks. This walk takes you along river paths and bridleways, which explore the edge of an ancient forest rewarding you with fine panoramic views of London.

The Royal Gunpowder Mills

On your meanderings through Lee Valley you might mention the gunpowder plot to the residents of Waltham Abbey and they may well return a quizzical look. Guy Fawkes might have procured some gunpowder hereabouts, but the only plot is the Royal Gunpowder Mills consisting of 175 acres (71ha) of parkland complete with 21 buildings and now a tourist attraction.

This walk takes you along the perimeter of the former 300-year-old gunpowder factory. Cut off from the urbanisation and development of the surrounding area, it became a wildlife haven and today boasts the biggest heronry in Essex. You will pass alder woods where trees once produced charcoal while in Galleyhill Wood, part of Epping Forest, you'll discover coppiced and pollarded trees.

Local Employer

Gunpowder was first manufactured here in the 1600s. In 1735 John Walton bought the Gunpowder Mill and his family churned out the stuff for the next 120 years. It was bought by the Crown in 1787 and became particularly handy during the Napoleonic Wars when production soared to 25,000 barrels a year. The factory sprawled across the Lee Valley and was connected by a complex network of canals to the Lee Valley Navigation and later by a railway to the arsenal and ammunition factory at Enfield. It also provided employment for local women during World War One before becoming an explosives research and development establishment.

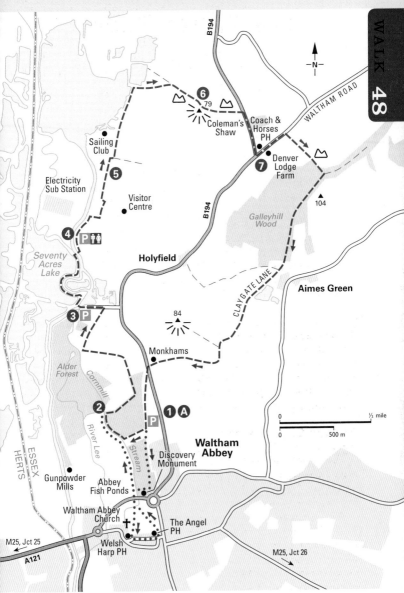

WALK 48 DIRECTIONS

❶ From the rear of the car park at Cornmill Meadows, take the gravel path to the information board and go straight ahead through woodland. At Cornmill Stream turn right with the stream down on your left-hand side and views across Cornmill Meadow.

At the footbridge turn right following the perimeter fence of the Waltham Abbey Royal Gunpowder Mills.

❷ Keep the fence on your left to a 'Hooks Marsh' fingerpost. The path then curves left across the field towards alder woodland. Turn right along the field-edge

WALK 48

path with the brook on your left, to a stile. Turn left on to Fishers Green Lane, which leads to a car park and information board.

3 Cross two footbridges over the streams and go through the kissing gate on the right signposted 'Fishers Green'. Follow the gravel path bounded by Seventy Acres Lake on the left.

4 After 600yds (549m) at the signposts indicating 'Lea Valley Park farms and Fishers Green', cross the metal footbridge and turn left through a picnic area. Follow the riverside path until you emerge at the tarmac road to a car park. Walk through this and turn left along a tarmac road to Fishers Green Sailing Club.

WHERE TO EAT AND DRINK

The Coach & Horses on the corner of St Leonard's Road makes a welcome stop for a pie and a pint. It's conveniently situated mid-way through this walk and if you sit at the outdoor tables you have fine views of Galleyhill Wood on the hill. Alternatively stock up on goodies and enjoy the waterside views at the picnic area at Seventy Acres Lake.

5 Pass Crannum Hide and just before the entrance of the sailing club turn right, cross a stile beside a gate and walk along the field-edge path keeping the sailing club on your left. Keep to the path as it bears right uphill to another stile.

6 At the top of the hill look back for wonderful views of north London and Hertfordshire. Follow the footpath sign for Clayton Hill, cross the wooden bridge and turn right to Coleman's Shaw. Turn right on to the B194 and follow the road as it goes downhill.

WHILE YOU'RE THERE

Visit the Royal Gunpowder Mills at Waltham Abbey for an explosive day out. You can create your own explosion through interactive computer displays, find out what it was like to work here or join a guided tour which includes wildlife watching from the tower and a visit to the largest heronry in Essex. This is one of the most important sites in Europe for the history of explosives and it is a must-see for those interested in industrial archaeology.

7 At the T-junction, turn left at the Coach & Horses pub into Waltham Road. Cross carefully and walk uphill past Denver Lodge Farm on the right. Cross the stile on the right and follow the field-edge path to Galleyhill Wood. Cross the next two stiles and continue, keeping the woods on your right, to the break in the trees. Walk through and at the cross path turn right on to the green lane to Galley Hill Green. Here, turn right and after 100yds (91m), turn left in front of houses to join Claygate Lane to emerge beside Eagle Lodge. Cross Crooked Mile Road to the meadow and turn left through the kissing gate and return to the car park.

WHAT TO LOOK OUT FOR

If it's a clear day and you're feeling adventurous and don't mind scrambling up the embankment of Claygate Lane Track on your way back to Cornmill Meadows car park you can treat yourself to some far-reaching views of London, including Canary Wharf and the television masts of Alexandra Palace.

Waltham Abbey

*Modern monuments, dragonfly-filled streams and
an ancient abbey.*

See map and information panel for Walk 48

DISTANCE 1.5 miles (2.4km) **MINIMUM TIME** 1hr
ASCENT/GRADIENT 269ft (82m) ▲▲▲ **LEVEL OF DIFFICULTY** ✦✦✦

WALK 49 DIRECTIONS
(Walk 48 option)

For a different start to Walk 48
at the car park, Point **Ⓐ**, turn
left at the end of the gravel path
and walk through the arboretum
where trees were grown to
supply London parks. After 0.5
mile (800m), cross two wooden
footbridges over the tributaries
of Cornmill Stream. Turn right
after the second bridge and after
150yds (137m) look out on your
left for the modern Discovery
monument, on the Greenwich
Meridian Line.

WHERE TO EAT AND DRINK
Pubs and eateries can be found
in Market Square and Sun Street,
but the most picturesque is the
Welsh Harp. Philpotts Tea Rooms,
on the green opposite Waltham
Abbey, has outdoor seating.

Cross the metal footbridge over
Cornmill Stream to the Dragonfly
Sanctuary and Abbey Fish Ponds.
Turn left under the B194 to
emerge on the grassy path leading
to another bridge over Cornmill
Stream. On your left are the
remains of Harold Bridge which
provided access for carts to the
abbey farmyard. You now have fine
views of the church of Waltham
Abbey to your right.

Founded in Saxon times as
a college, in 1066 it became
the burial place of King
Harold. Henry II established
an Augustinian priory here, as
penance for Thomas Becket's
murder. It was raised to abbey
status in 1184 and was the last to
be dissolved by Henry VIII. All
that remains of the abbey is the
Great West Tower and nave, now
Waltham Abbey church.

WHILE YOU'RE THERE
Call in at the free Epping Forest
District Museum located in a
16th-century building in Sun
Street for an insight into life in
the area from the Stone Age
through to modern times.

At the Abbey Church Centre, on
your left, turn right and follow the
path via the Cloister archway and
through the coaching entrance of
the Welsh Harp pub into Market
Place. Turn left into Sun Street
and left again after The Angel pub
passing the rear of shops to the
break in the abbey walls. From
here return to the Dragonfly
Sanctuary, keeping the stream on
your right for 0.5 mile (800m).
Cross the bridge and turn left to
join Walk 48 at Point **Ⓑ** or turn
right to return to the car park.

Theydon Bois to the End of the Line

A linear walk overground to the underground crossing the M25 tunnel.

WALK 50

DISTANCE 4 miles (6.4km)   **MINIMUM TIME** 1hr 30min

ASCENT/GRADIENT 217ft (66m) ▲▲▲   **LEVEL OF DIFFICULTY** ✚✚✚

PATHS Forest and grassy tracks, some urban streets

LANDSCAPE Undulating ancient forestland, common and town views

SUGGESTED MAP OS Explorer 174 Epping Forest & Lee Valley

START Grid reference: TQ 455991   **FINISH** Grid reference: TL 462016

DOG FRIENDLINESS Dog-friendly woodlands and welcoming watering holes, can be off lead in forest

PARKING Pay-and-display at Theydon Bois and Epping underground stations. Free off-street parking by The Green, Theydon Bois

PUBLIC TOILETS Theydon Bois and Epping underground stations visit www.firstgreatwestern.co.uk

---

WALK 50 DIRECTIONS

Many parts of Epping Forest are well used, yet as the largest open space in the vicinity of London and Essex it is still possible to find tranquil niches even during the height of summer. One of these areas is in the northern reaches of the forest at Theydon Bois, where you don't even need your car to get there, as the area is well served by the underground. This walk takes you through the forest to emerge at the little town of Epping. Just 17 miles (27.4km) north-east of London and at the end of the Central Line.

Turn left outside Theydon Bois underground station, passing the Railway Arms and The Bull, into Coppice Row. Continue uphill passing The Green on your left and the Queen Victoria pub on your right. Cross Piercing Hill and soon afterwards you pass the Theydon Bois schoolhouse, built in 1840, followed by St Mary The

Virgin church with its delightful porch inscribed, 'There is no death'. Pause a moment here to admire the oak tree and the war memorial in the graveyard.

Coppice Row changes its name to become Jack's Hill, named after Jack Rann, a most notorious highwayman who robbed anything that moved. He was nicknamed 'Sixteen String Jack', because he appeared at the Old Bailey with 'sixteen coloured ribbons streaming from the knees of his breeches'. In Jack's Hill, the

---

WHERE TO EAT AND DRINK

There is no shortage of eateries on this route. Fill up on the all day breakfast at the Railway Inn at Theydon Bois or lunch at the Bull next door. In Epping High Street choose from the Duke of Wellington or tuck into fish and chips at the adjacent Smith's restaurant. There's also the Half Moon and the George & Dragon and tea shops and cafés galore.

WHAT TO LOOK OUT FOR

Epping High Street is a Conservation Area with many listed buildings dating back to the 18th century. Some of the oldest are an attractive group of 17th- and 18th-century cottages at Nos 98 to 110. Look for the plaque on the Co-op building, once the site of much electioneering by Sir Winston Churchill (1874–1965), before he became Prime Minister.

Sixteen String Jack pub, complete with inn sign, shows the grinning rogue preparing to meet his death at the gallows.

After the church, walk 200yds (183m) and turn right beside a barrier. Follow the path left through the forest, now walking uphill parallel with Jack's Hill. In among the trees and ditches you can picture a posse of highwaymen plotting their next robbery as stage coaches would speed their way along the main London road to and from Aldgate.

Continue uphill with the B172 a few paces away on your left. At the cross path, with the car park on your left, go straight on, and at the next car park turn right on to the path. This is the Green Ride bridleway from Epping to Loughton. Keep to the main path, which is bounded by coppiced oak and hornbeams, many with gnarled trunks and grotesque shapes, which all add to the sinister atmosphere of the area.

The path dips after 0.5 mile (800m), where to the left through woodland is a sign indicating the Iron Age earthworks at Ambresbury Banks. Legend has it that Queen Boudicca fought her last battle against the Romans here but there is little evidence to

support this story. Continue along the main forest path and you will see evidence of the 1987 storm damage, during which many trees were brought down. At the end of the ride, where the path curves sharply right, keep ahead and bear half right following bridleway markers across grassland to Theydon Road. Turn left past Ivy Chimneys Road on your right and walk towards Bell Common.

As you cross Ivy Chimneys Road, look right and in the distance you can see vehicles on the M25 seemingly emerging from the ground beneath your feet. During the building of the busy M25 motorway in the 1980s, it was proposed to route the M25 over Bell Common. Fierce opposition from local citizens, forest lovers and the Conservators of Epping Forest resulted in a tunnel for the traffic, which has preserved the area we are walking on today.

Pass the Forest Gate Inn on your right and cross Bell Common Road with its attractive 18th-century cottages and houses, into Epping by turning right along the grassy path across the common with the High Road close on your left. Cross Hemnall Street, join the pavement, and you will see the water tower, built in 1872, one of three tower landmarks which stand on a ridge of the main road and which can be seen for many miles around.

At the mini-roundabout by the church continue along the attractive High Street to explore its weather-boarded cottages, cafés and shop fronts. Otherwise turn right along Station Road and continue downhill to Epping underground station – the end of the Central Line.

Walking in Safety

All these walks are suitable for any reasonably fit person, but less experienced walkers should try the easier walks first. Route finding is usually straightforward, but you will find that an Ordnance Survey map is a useful addition to the route maps and descriptions.

RISKS

Although each walk here has been researched with a view to minimising the risks to the walkers who follow its route, no walk in the countryside can be considered to be completely free from risk. Walking in the outdoors will always require a degree of common sense and judgement to ensure that it is as safe as possible.

- Be particularly careful on cliff paths and in upland terrain, where the consequences of a slip can be very serious.

- Remember to check tidal conditions before walking on the seashore.

- Some sections of route are by, or cross, busy roads. Take care and remember traffic is a danger even on minor country lanes.

- Be careful around farmyard machinery and livestock, especially if you have children with you.

- Be aware of the consequences of changes in the weather and check the forecast before you set out. Carry spare clothing and a torch if you are walking in the winter months. Remember the weather can change very quickly at any time of the year, and in moorland and heathland areas, mist and fog can make route finding much harder. Don't set out in these conditions unless you are confident of your navigation skills in poor visibility. In summer remember to take account of the heat and sun; wear a hat and carry spare water.

- On walks away from centres of population you should carry a whistle and survival bag. If you do have an accident requiring the emergency services, make a note of your position as accurately as possible and dial 999.

COUNTRYSIDE CODE

- Be safe, plan ahead and follow any signs.

- Leave gates and property as you find them.

- Protect plants and animals and take your litter home.

- Keep dogs under close control.

- Consider other people.

For more information visit www.countrysideaccess.gov.uk/things_to_know/countryside_code